"MUST READING FOR EVERY MEMBER OF THE ACCOUNTING PROFESSION . . .
For the lay person, it should help to remove some of the mystery surrounding the accounting profession."
—Robert D. Thorne, Vice President and Controller, U.S.G. Corporation

"If accounting is the 'language of business,' this will be a very useful guide for anyone who speaks it."
—Russell Palmer, Dean, The Wharton School

"EXCELLENT COVERAGE OF TODAY'S CHALLENGES AND CONTROVERSIES."
—John R. Meinert, Chairman, Hartmarx Corporation

"An accurate and insightful look at a profession in a white-water period and how it is emerging as a more significant and vibrant force in our free-enterprise society."
—Edward A. Kangas, Managing Partner, Touche Ross & Co.

"RECOMMENDED . . . A thoughtful overview of a profession that has come in for increasing outside attention."
—Library Journal

"THIS SUPERB DISCUSSION of the past, present and future in the accounting world provides a real basis for developing strategies for firms and individuals alike."
—Roscoe Egger, Partner, Price Waterhouse, Former IRS Commissioner

GRACE W. WEINSTEIN, a nationally syndicated newspaper columnist and contributing editor/consultant for *Ms.* magazine, writes for a wide array of national magazines, from *Money* to *McCall's,* and is a lecturer and consultant on personal finance. Among her previously published books are *The Lifetime Book of Money Management, Children and Money: A Guide for Parents,* and *Men, Women & Money: New Roles, New Rules.*

OTHER BOOKS BY GRACE W. WEINSTEIN

CHILDREN AND MONEY: A Parent's Guide

THE LIFETIME BOOK OF MONEY MANAGEMENT

MEN, WOMEN & MONEY: New Roles, New Rules

THE
BOTTOM LINE

Inside Accounting Today

Grace W. Weinstein

A PLUME BOOK

NEW AMERICAN LIBRARY

A DIVISION OF PENGUIN BOOKS USA INC.

NEW YORK

PUBLISHED IN CANADA BY
PENGUIN BOOKS CANADA LIMITED, MARKHAM, ONTARIO

To the memory of
Stanley H. Beckerman, CPA,
an admirable resource,
a scholar and a gentleman

NAL BOOKS ARE AVAILABLE AT QUANTITY DISCOUNTS WHEN USED
TO PROMOTE PRODUCTS OR SERVICES. FOR INFORMATION PLEASE
WRITE TO PREMIUM MARKETING DIVISION, NEW AMERICAN LIBRARY,
1633 BROADWAY, NEW YORK, NEW YORK 10019.

The Bottom Line previously appeared in an NAL BOOKS edition published by New
American Library and in Canada by the New American Library of Canada Limited
(now Penguin Books Canada Limited).

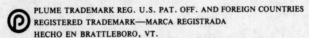

PLUME TRADEMARK REG. U.S. PAT. OFF. AND FOREIGN COUNTRIES
REGISTERED TRADEMARK—MARCA REGISTRADA
HECHO EN BRATTLEBORO, VT.

SIGNET, SIGNET CLASSIC, MENTOR, ONYX, PLUME, MERIDIAN
and NAL BOOKS are published *in the United States* by
New American Library, a division of Penguin Books USA, Inc.,
1633 Broadway, New York, New York 10019,
in Canada by Penguin Books Canada Limited,
2801 John Street, Markham, Ontario L3R 1B4

Library of Congress Cataloging-in-Publication Data
Weinstein, Grace W.
   The bottom line.
   1. Accounting—United States. I. Title.
HF5616. U5W44   1987   657   87-11228
ISBN 0-453-00563-2
ISBN 0-452-26240-2 (pbk.)

First Plume Printing, April, 1989

1 2 3 4 5 6 7 8 9

PRINTED IN THE UNITED STATES OF AMERICA

Contents

Introduction

"I eat lobster like an accountant," my friend said, in response to her husband's comment that she was the slowest one at the table. Everyone laughed. But, in fact, Judy meant that she was being methodical, meticulous, painstaking in her attack on the crustacean.

Judy isn't a CPA. But her perception is probably close to universal. Certified public acountants have a well-deserved reputation for paying attention to detail. The accounting profession has emerged in survey after survey as a highly thought-of profession, its practitioners respected for their integrity, their objectivity, their competence. But these qualities can also imply being literal-minded and doing things "by the book," a perception confirmed in a 1986 survey by Louis Harris and Associates, which revealed that certified public accountants don't score particularly high on creativity. This can be a good thing; "creative accounting" has a very negative implication when it comes to corporate financial statements. But certified public accountants are performing more and more management advisory services, services designed to help companies grow and prosper, services in which creativity is vital.

So Judy's perception of CPAs, while accurate, is incomplete. Today's CPAs perform a variety of functions and come with an increasing variety of temperaments. Yet the general public, even the educated public, seems to have a view of the CPA's role that is as narrow as this common

1

perception of the CPA's personality. Ask the average person what an accountant does, and you're likely to get a one-word response: taxes. Ask a corporate executive or a financial analyst or an investor, and the response may be audit.

Accountants are, of course, closely associated with taxes and with audits. But they do far, far more. Management accountants are engaged in a wide range of jobs within corporate America. Public accounting firms are involved in a variety of activities, from strategic business planning to designing and developing computer systems to executive financial planning. In their myriad roles, CPAs are playing an increasingly vital role in American business. And as business becomes internationalized, the practice of accounting becomes increasingly internationalized as well.

Perhaps it's not surprising that the winds of change are sweeping the profession. Services are becoming increasingly diversified, to a point where some proffered services seem far removed from the profession's traditional areas of expertise. CPAs are competing among themselves and, increasingly, with non-CPA providers of similar services. Amidst such competition, charges of underbidding and other unprofessional behavior proliferate. As competition increases, moreover, many public accounting firms are turning to marketing efforts that are new to CPAs, including advertising and public relations, to augment traditional forms of practice development. In this marketing, some firms, to the chagrin of others, are as likely to call themselves management consultants as certified public accountants.

But that's not all. Some observers believe that some types of management advisory services, when performed for audit clients, may compromise auditor independence. Perhaps even more important, auditors have been challenged about the issuance of "clean" opinions about a company's financial statements followed, sometimes all too quickly, by business failure. Mounting legal liability is an increasingly contentious issue. Congress, for the second time in ten years, is conducting hearings into the profession and considering government regulation. The organized profession, conscious of its own image, is beefing up self-regulatory efforts.

Technological advances, meanwhile, are changing what CPAs do and how they do it, with resulting changes in the traditional structure of firms. Education and career tracks are being scrutinized and may well be modified to meet the changing needs of a changing profession.

As the organized accounting profession in the United States celebrates its centennial year, it seems appropriate to examine these and other issues critical to the profession and, in turn, to American business. The American Institute of Certified Public Accountants (AICPA) has asked me to evaluate the profession in light of these issues and of its general impact on American life in these last decades of the twentieth century. It has given me a free journalistic hand in my investigation, offering only the research assistance and cooperation I've requested. My thanks go to the staff of the Institute, particularly Helene Kennedy, and to the approximately 125 people I interviewed, in many parts of the United States, both inside and outside the profession. Their contributions, in data and insight, have been invaluable. My observations and conclusions, however, must stand on their own.

1

Accountants and Accountability: An Overview

"This is a white-water time, and the staid old profession is right in the middle of the wild currents, dealing with it reasonably well," says Edward A. Kangas, managing partner of Touche Ross. "Accounting is still very attractive to an awful lot of the best and the brightest. They view it as vibrant because it may be that, while we're in troubled times in some ways, it's a lot more exciting than it was twenty-five years ago."

Accounting has existed almost from the beginning of recorded time. It may not, at the outset, have gone by the name "accounting," but at least since the first merchants started trading goods and the first caravans wended their way across the sands of Middle Eastern deserts, people have kept accounts. How many camels did X trade to Y? Did Y pay in full for the transaction? Is a camel or two owing on the deal? Accounting provided the necessary answers, in a universal language that has been called the language of business.

Today, accounting still provides the necessary answers and is still the international language of business. Accountants may use computers instead of abacuses, but they still track business transactions and provide a historical record of those transactions. Business may deal with petrochemicals instead of camels, but auditors still review financial statements and attest to the accuracy of those statements.

As business has become more complex, so, too, has the work that accountants do.

But accounting and attestation are only part of the picture. Today's certified public accountants—accountants who have passed a uniform nationwide examination and have been licensed by their states to practice public accounting—perform a multitude of functions. Skilled in cash flow projections, expert in tax law, knowledgeable about personal and business needs, respected for their independence and their integrity, CPAs are playing an ever-greater role in day-to-day life. Even if you haven't personally used the services of a CPA, chances are good that you will sometime in the future or that, in any case, your life will be touched in some way by the work that CPAs do.

If you are covered by a company pension plan, for example, the amount of pension you will actually receive is governed in part by the accounting standards pertaining to pension funds. If you invest in the stock market, your potential profit—or loss—is determined in part by the way the corporation, within generally accepted accounting principles, reports its earnings. If you are a taxpayer, the amount you must pay in taxes is directly affected by government accounting practices and the efficiency of audits of government expenditures.

On a more immediate level, you might turn to a CPA for help with a wide range of personal questions. For example:

- Nearing retirement, Eric faces several decisions: Should he take his company pension in a lump sum or in monthly installments? Is a reduced pension with survivor's benefits the wisest choice, or should he take a full pension and protect his wife with life insurance? If he retires early, can he maintain his desired standard of living for a lifetime? Using cash flow projections, with interest rate and inflation rate assumptions, Eric's CPA does what Stanley Breitbard, national director of

Executive Financial Services for Price Waterhouse, calls a retirement sufficiency analysis. "We look at current assets, income, anticipated retirement benefits, and determine how much income will be generated." If it's not enough to support his lifestyle for his life expectancy at early retirement, Eric has to make some choices: retire later, accept a reduced standard of living, or, perhaps, accept a bit more investment risk in the interest of greater return.

- As young parents, Jane and Jerry ponder some serious financial questions: What's the best way to set aside money for college? How should they structure their estates to minimize any potential tax bite? Again, their CPA does a cash flow projection to determine how much they should save each month to be ready for their newborn's freshman year of college. She also suggests that estate taxes will not be a concern at their asset level; estate planning should focus, instead, on appropriate guardianship and custodianship provisions for their children.

- With her marriage splintering, Angela needs help. How can she find out about assets her husband may have kept in his own name and concealed from her? How can she get the best possible property settlement? Should she sell the house or try to keep it? Her estranged husband, on the other hand, wants to protect his assets and maintain his standard of living. Here, Jeff Saccacio, national director of Personal Financial Planning for KMG Main Hurdman,* suggests that cash flow considerations are as important as tax consideration. "I had one case in which the proposed agreement looked good from a tax standpoint but, in terms

---

*On April 1, 1987, KMG Main Hurdman merged with Peat Marwick Mitchell & Co., a merger described in Chapter 8. For purposes of identification, however, individuals who were with either KMG Main Hurdman or Peat Marwick Mitchell when they were interviewed for this book are so identified throughout.

of cash flow, my client would have been stripped bare. They renegotiated.''

- Phil, still single and just a few years out of college, is beginning to earn a sizable income and thinks he should start investing, but he's not quite sure which way to go. Are tax-free investments such as municipal bonds appropriate for him? What about a limited partnership? Would he be better off seeking capital growth in the stock market? Most CPAs don't recommend specific investments, but they can help clients decide on an investment strategy and point to appropriate investment categories to help implement that strategy. More important than any particular investment, perhaps, is forced savings on a regular basis. "With young clients," says Joel S. Isaacson, manager of financial planning for Weber, Lipshie & Co. in New York City, "I try to get them into a monthly investment program. If the mortgage is due on the first then they should invest on the fifteenth. And they should invest for the long term. The rate of investing is far more important, in my opinion, than the rate of return."

- Ann's home-based word processing business has done very well, so well that she is expanding her staff and taking a storefront location near the county courthouse. Should she remain a sole proprietor? Or should she consider a corporate structure? Either way, what kind of benefits should she offer her staff? What taxes must she pay on their behalf? With the Tax Reform Act of 1986, Ann's CPA points out, for the first time in many years the corporate income tax is generally higher than the personal income tax. Ann should stick to a sole proprietorship, a partnership, or, perhaps, the special Subchapter S form of corporation.

- Ed's auto parts shop is also doing well. But, as Ed prepares to apply for an expansion loan, he realizes that he needs a computer system to track parts and orders. What kind of system will do the job in the most cost-effective manner? What software is tailored to his business needs? His CPA provides the answers, while also compiling financial statements for the loan application and helping Ed prepare a presentation to answer the loan officer's questions.

With Ann and Ed, we're moving from personal problems into the realm of business problems. CPAs, knowing their clients and their clients' businesses, can tackle and help to resolve a whole host of concerns. They work with both large and small firms. In fact, says Philip Chenok, president of the AICPA, "The smaller the business, the greater the need. Large businesses have their in-house experts." For example:

- When two partners opened an athletic-shoe-store franchise in a midwestern city, their CPA helped them set up an accounting system, showed them how to prepare monthly financial statements, and introduced budgeting techniques. She also prepared their tax returns and, as the business grew, helped to computerize the inventory system.
- An owner of a privately held construction company was ready to retire and turn the business over to his son but wanted to maintain an income stream from the business. He turned to his accountant, who suggested recapitalizing the business. The father converted his stock into dividend-paying preferred stock, which froze the father's interest in the business while providing income. The common stock went to the son, as an incentive to make the business grow.

But large firms do also use the expertise of accounting firms, as do government entities:

- The executives of a major corporation wanted to streamline operations by improving employee productivity. The public accounting firm hired as a consultant recommended an employee recruitment-and-hiring system that went from recruitment procedures through personnel training and performance evaluations to salary incentive programs and retirement planning. Costs were cut by eliminating duplicative functions. Productivity increased, and employee morale improved.

• When a prison system was faced with severe overcrowding, the off-the-cuff official response was to build more prisons. The CPA firm called in as consultants, however, had another approach: Find out why the overcrowding occurs. Its study revealed that a great many cell occupants were ineligible for bail and awaiting trial for long periods of time. The solution: Hire more staff to speed the process from date of arrest to date of judgment.

This multiplicity of problems and solutions demonstrates the multitude of roles today's CPAs play. Yet these examples are just the tip of the iceberg. In public practice, as we've seen, CPAs answer both personal and business needs ranging from college funding to computer installation to strategic planning. Some work in audit and accounting, some in tax, some in management advisory services. Some specialize in such areas as personal financial planning and mangement information systems. Some specialize by industry, with expertise in health care or retailing or restaurants or the nonprofit sector.

But not all CPAs are engaged in public practice. Within business and industry they work as chief financial officers, corporate treasurers and controllers, internal auditors, and a host of other positions. These CPAs are responsible for developing and analyzing information needed for business decisions. They evaluate the financial effects of proposed management actions. And they prepare the reports issued for use by lenders and investors. One CPA in industry, for example, is vice-president, finance and administration, for a major utility. His responsibilities include supervising the accounting department, accumulating and analyzing all of the company's financial data, monitoring and updating operating systems, coordinating audit work with internal auditors and outside auditors, developing and monitoring budgets, and maintaining relationships with lenders. Another CPA, an internal auditor in a manufacturing concern, evaluates and reports to management on the effectiveness of the organization's operations and systems, recommending corrective actions needed to reduce unnecessary costs and improve internal controls.

As defined by the National Association of Accountants (NAA), an organization of some ninety-five thousand professional (but not necessarily certified) accountants, "Management accounting is the process of identification, measurement, accumulation, analysis, preparation, interpretation, and communication of financial information used by management to plan, evaluate, and control within an organization and to assure use of and accountability for its resources. Management accounting also comprises the preparation of financial reports for nonmanagement groups such as shareholders, creditors, regulatory agencies, and tax authorities."

In government, CPAs perform as auditors, bank examiners, inspectors general, budget officers. In one state government, for instance, a CPA serves as director of the department of revenue, advising the governor and the legislature on tax policy issues. He also manages the department's statewide programs, including statewide property appraisal and assessment, child support enforcement, and, not least, a wholesale and retail liquor distribution system. In a major East Coast city, a CPA is administrator of internal audit, engaging independent auditors and arranging for the audit of hundreds of citywide programs. Some CPAs reach very high levels in government: for example, the current Comptroller General of the United States, Charles Bowsher, and the immediate past Commissioner of Internal Revenue, Roscoe L. Egger, Jr.

Other CPAs are in the academic community. As faculty members at colleges and universities, they prepare students for accounting careers. They design new courses and curricula to meet the profession's ever-changing educational needs, counsel students about accounting careers, and conduct research to expand the body of accounting knowledge. Current research includes investigations into how accounting and auditing information is used to make decisions, examinations of how the behavioral sciences can aid the understanding of the way in which accountants and auditors perform their tasks, and studies about the effectiveness of auditing techniques in the examination of financial statements.

Public Accounting Today

While CPAs in industry, government, and academia fulfill vital jobs, most of the issues swirling around the field of accounting today focus on public accounting. That's because the CPA acting as an independent auditor is viewed as putting a seal of approval on what others have done, a seal critical to both investors and lenders and hence to the functioning of our capitalist economy. And there are a surprising number of serious issues for what has been considered a staid old profession. "The number-one complaint of CPAs thirty years ago was that nobody paid attention to us," says Gordon Scheer, executive director of the Colorado State Society of CPAs. "Today our complaint would be that we're getting too much attention. We're on the hot seat."

Actually, it's not such a new phenomenon for attention to be paid the accounting profession. Accountants have been in the limelight before. There has been controversy over small matters, such as the introduction of looseleaf ledgers in the late nineteenth century; this great leap forward from the earlier cumbersome bound ledgers (when allocated pages were used up, entries were continued a confusing fifty or eighty-seven or a hundred pages farther on) was construed as an invitation to fraud. And controversy has centered on larger matters, with instances of corporate fraud, as in the McKesson & Robbins case of the 1930's, raising cries of "Where were the auditors?"

But, despite their feeling of being "on the hot seat," CPAs today are generally seen in a very favorable light. "The accounting profession is among the best-regarded institutions in the country," according to the 1986 Harris survey cited earlier. "In an era when misdeeds of the powerful are trumpeted in daily headlines, it's difficult for any profession to earn public trust," Lou Harris told the AICPA Council in October 1986. "It's no mean accomplishment for CPAs to emerge at the top." Among all the surveyed groups, CPAs measured up well in their ethical and moral practices. They ranked extremely high in honesty, competence, reliability, and objectivity. Despite these findings, though, there's little doubt that the current spotlight of attention is both brighter and more sharply focused than it has been in the past. The accounting profession, as a result, must focus its own attention on several significant areas.

The Auditor's Role

The world's capital markets rely on financial statements certified by independent auditors. If the integrity of those statements could not be trusted, investment would come to a halt and economic growth would be paralyzed.

Yet questions have been raised about whether recent business failures, some linked to management fraud, are in fact audit failures. When a business goes belly-up shortly after auditors have rendered an unqualified opinion (an opinion without reservations), critics question whether the auditors have done their job properly. When management engages in fraud and investors lose their shirts, critics ask why the auditors didn't catch the fraud and signal a warning.

Concerned about many recent business failures, Congress, for the second time in ten years, has put the spotlight on the accounting profession and its practices. In Congressman John D. Dingell's words, in *New Accountant* magazine, "It became imperative that Congress investigate the role of the accounting profession, as we saw repeated revelations of illegal conduct of corporate officers, bank failures leading to huge government bailouts, and a series of stock manipulations and conglomerate takeovers that were apparently accomplished with the aid of accounting gimmicks." The House Subcommittee on Oversight and Investigations of the Committee on Energy and Commerce (the Dingell Committee) has raised two basic issues: "The first is the sharp contrast between the accounting firms' view of their professional responsibilities and the higher expectations generally held by the public with respect to independent auditors. . . . The second basic theme behind the issues is the SEC's wholesale delegation of its rulemaking and enforcement authority to private accounting organizations." The hearings are not yet over, at this writing, but the congressional message to the profession seems clear: Mend your ways, or government regulation is a distinct possibility.

What's at issue may be less what auditors do, as the committee states, than the public's often mistaken perception of what they do. The auditor's opinion states only that management's financial statements have been fairly presented in accordance with generally accepted accounting principles. In doing so it presents a snapshot of the financial position of the company at a particular moment. The opinion does not promise that the company will continue as a profitable going concern. CPAs say that investors and lenders need to go beyond the financial statements in making their decisions. But the public, by and large, views an unqualified auditor's opinion as a clean bill of health. Lawsuits have been filed over the issue.

The Harris survey asked several key questions about

the public's understanding of audits. It found that two out of three people (leadership groups are more sophisticated) consider a "clean" opinion to mean that the auditor judges management to be doing a competent job. And about half believe that a "clean" opinion means that the auditor certifies the company as a good investment. Auditors, in fact, do not attest to the competence of management. And auditors do not, and will not, certify any company as a good investment.

There's a real difference, in short, between the way auditors perceive their roles and the way Congress and the general public appear to perceive them. This "expectation gap" has to be addressed and is being addressed within the accounting profession. Major changes have been proposed in auditing standards; the "going concern" question is likely to be addressed as a company's condition is reported in the annual report, and fraud is more likely to be sought out and, if detected, reported to the highest levels of management. "We have to narrow the gap by improving our performance," says 1986-87 AICPA chairman Michael J. Cook, "expanding the usefulness of financial statements, particularly in providing early warning of business risk."

Financial reporting improprieties, of course, go beyond auditors' reports. The National Commission on Fraudulent Financial Reporting, sponsored by the AICPA, the National Association of Accountants, the Financial Executives Institute, the Institute of Internal Auditors, and the American Accounting Association, is suggesting broad-based changes in corporate and auditor behavior to reduce the likelihood of fraud.

Government Audits

When it comes to audits of government funds, it's another ball game. Government audits have rules of their own, requiring that auditors not only certify the financial statements but certify that expenditures comply with government laws and regulations. Critics assert that many accountants are inadequately prepared for the complexity of government audits. Others say that some accountants cut corners in submitting competitive bids and then cut corners in doing the job to come in under bid. And many CPAs claim that governmental entities are interested only in low bids, not good audits. Whatever the reasons, fully one-third of government audits have been reported to be substandard, and a congressional committee (the Brooks Committee) is conducting an investigation.

Accountants themselves admit that substandard reporting is not uncommon. At a recent meeting in Colorado, for example, most of the seventy or so accountants in the room said they had seen substandard work. The Utah Association of CPAs, in another instance, notes that "some practitioners are not complying with accepted professional standards in order to reduce costs and gain competitive advantage."

But the profession is tackling this issue head-on, introducing both continuing education courses specializing in government audits and a quality review program. Both should raise the quality of government audits, and help to protect the taxpayers' dollar.

Scope of Services

Part of the attention the profession is receiving these days stems directly from its multiplicity of roles. CPAs don't branch out into new areas of practice without controversy. As far back as 1925, historian Gary John Previts points out in *The Scope of CPA Services* (1986), there was debate about the proper extent of accountants' practice. Those considered "eccentric" were aggressive, ready to explore new fields; those described as "concentric" were conservative, sticking to their tradititional past.

Today this division, although without these labels, still

exists. Those we might call traditionalists focus on audit, tax, and management advisory services. Those we could term ground-breakers expand management consulting into a wide range of service areas, from executive financial planning to corporate facilities planning. The real question—in fact, almost the only question—is whether management consulting in all its ramifications jeopardizes auditor independence.

The fact is that the three main services provided by accountants today demand different standards and have different and conflicting characteristics. As put by the AICPA Special Committee on Standards of Professional Conduct for Certified Public Accountants (known as the Anderson Committee, after its chairman, George D. Anderson of Anderson Zur Muehler & Co. in Helena, Montana), "Audits of financial statements require objectivity and independence. Consulting requires professional objectivity but does not require independence. And providing tax services often requires CPAs to support interpretations most favorable to their clients while maintaining professional objectivity. The contemporaneous performance of these services may place a CPA in conflicting roles."

Conflicting roles or no, many people think that it's okay for accountants to perform management advisory services—after all, who better to turn to for business advice than the person who knows your business so well?—but that they have no business in facilities planning, for example, or in identifying merger and acquisition candidates.

The nay-sayers, however, are overwhelmed by events. CPAs *are* expanding their services to meet the expanding needs of their clients. That expansion is unlikely to stop. But it needs to be measured, and will be measured, in terms of maintaining CPAs' well-deserved reputation for independence and integrity.

Competition

Competitive bidding, as noted above, is common in government audits. But fee-based competition—considered unprofessional by many—is rearing its head across the spectrum of accounting services. Government pressure in the late 1970's led to the elimination of professional restrictions on advertising. That opened the door not only to advertising but to such scorned practices as underbidding or "lowballing," a practice that is intensified by the merger trend that has reduced the number of publicly traded corporate clients.

The accounting profession, unlike any other, is characterized by a chasm between large and small firms. There is a handful of extraordinarily large firms at the top (the "Big Eight" plus a few other large national firms), with thousands and thousands of employees. The number-one firm in size, newly born of a merger between Peat Marwick Mitchell and KMG Main Hurdman, has about 20,000 employees in the United States and some 58,000 worldwide. At the other end of the spectrum are thousands of sole practitioners. In between are regional firms and local firms. Of the approximately 120,000 AICPA members in public practice in 1986 (no one is quite sure how many CPAs do not belong to AICPA), 25 percent were in 1-member firms, 34.3 percent in firms of 2 to 9 members, 15 percent in firms with 10 or more members (excepting the twenty-five largest firms), and 25.6 percent in those twenty-five largest firms.

The major national firms are known for their audits of major publicly held companies and for the breadth of their management advisory services. The smallest firms, for the most part, emphasize personal attention to small businesses and individual taxpayers. The mid-size firms typically carve out a market niche in which they perform a variety of services.

But the major firms, losing audit clients in the wake of

corporate mergers, are expanding their efforts to reach small business. They're also moving into new areas by absorbing smaller firms. Today big firms are at each other's throats, little firms see big firms coming after their small-business clients, and middle-sized firms, some fear, are being squeezed out of existence. They're not really being squeezed out; AICPA statistics show the largest growth in this area. But the perception isn't totally unfounded, though. "The medium-size firm has the most pressure on it right now, in terms of costs," says Martin Rosenberg, executive director of the Illinois CPA Society, "because it's expected to provide most of the services of the large firms. It also needs all of the resources, the library, major computer systems, lots of administrative support, quality review personnel."

Some observers forecast an increasing polarization between large national firms and small local "boutique" firms. We're really "talking about two professions, one to serve public clients and the other to serve middle America, if you will," notes John C. Burton, dean of the Graduate School of Business at Columbia University, "and they have some very competing interests." Certainly, as the Institute's Report of the Special Committee on Small and Medium-Sized Firms (the Derieux Committee) put it in 1980 (and little has changed since), "the environment in which smaller, privately held businesses operate is different from that of larger publicly held companies." As client companies differ, so do their CPAs. Whatever happens as firms shake out—and it's still too early to be sure—today's competitive pressures make accounting a far cry from the sedate profession of yesteryear.

Education

With the redefining of the audit function and the proliferation of other services, together with an explosion of information on all fronts, the education of accountants is receiving a good hard look in many quarters. Right now, the CPA certificate is based (with slight variations from state to state) on a four-year college degree, a year or two of experience in public accounting, and a passing grade on the CPA exam.

These requirements are under study, with a growing movement toward mandatory postgraduate education. Three states currently require a fifth year of education, and the AICPA is pushing for this requirement on a national basis. But not everyone agrees. While proponents point to the fact that accounting is the only major profession that does not require advanced education and that broad-based education is essential in today's business environment, opponents assert that (a) advanced education isn't really necessary and (b) it would be a barrier to disadvantaged individuals seeking advancement through a profession.

Advanced education or not, the profession is facing a serious question of how to attract the best college graduates. In an era when investment banking is the glamor field (although now perhaps somewhat sullied by the recent insider trading scandals), accounting must develop ways to attract and to keep top students.

What can the public realistically expect from independent auditors? Are there boundaries to the services CPAs can legitimately perform? How much education do they need to perform them? In order to put such questions into perspective, to trace accounting's development as the universal language of business, we need to look back a bit into the past.

Where It All Began

Accounting is both a very new and a very old profession. Contemporary accounting can even be said to have two beginnings. Depending on your point of view, it began in the late nineteenth century in Great Britain, with the examiners of accounts who called themselves chartered accountants. Or it began in 1933, in the United States, when the first Securities Acts required that corporate books be audited by independent auditors. Either way, the profession's antecedents go back much further.

Accounting in the form of record-keeping has existed as long as human beings have been conducting commerce. As far back as 4500 B.C., the Babylonians and Assyrians had a system of accounting; clay tablets recording receipts and disbursements have been found going back to at least 3000 B.C. In ancient Greece, citizens were appointed to review the accounts of government officials; these accounts were engraved on stone and put on public display. Later, the Romans developed sophisticated methods of collecting taxes, disbursing payroll, and keeping records. Roman bookkeepers and clerks had an added incentive to be accurate in their review of government accounts: They received a percentage on the amount of mistakes and frauds that they detected (not a farfetched idea, perhaps, since it came close to revival in the 1986 Tax Act with a proposed trust fund for the IRS). And Robert L. Hagerman of the School of Management, State University of New York at Buffalo, notes in an article in the *Journal of Accountancy* that the Bible has a number of references, both direct and indirect, to financial accounting, internal controls, and, to a lesser extent, management accounting in the form of project budgeting and cash flow forecasts.

Although accounting became increasingly sophisticated with the invention of double-entry bookkeeping in Italy in the fifteenth century, and the Old World–New World trade of the colonial era, accountants were still considered essentially "examiners of accounts." And interesting accounts many were: The Pilgrims were audited by the men who raised the money for their trip. The jailers of the Salem witches, on trial in the 1690's, kept accounts of their expenditures. Benjamin Franklin used a representative to tally a business debt in 1748.

Yet accounting itself, as Previts points out, and as legions of accountants over the centuries can verify, remained identified in the public mind with the "musty drudgery" of record-keeping and record review. This musty drudgery may be a thing of the past, as far as today's CPAs are concerned, but the public image lingers. Green computer screens have long since replaced green eyeshades, computer software has taken over much of the repetitive detail work of audits, and CPAs engage in many activities besides audits, but most people still have very little idea of just what accountants actually do.

Accounts were kept in America from the earliest colonial days. But the modern era of accountancy is usually said to have begun with the chartered accountants of Great Britain, professionals who went beyond record-keeping and record review to investigate the affairs of business and disclose those affairs to investors. This audit function, emerging along with the prototype of the modern corporation and its multiple shareholder owners, was brought to the United States by British accountants in the late nineteenth century.

There had been homegrown accountants prior to the 1880's, as we've seen, but they functioned primarily as bookkeepers, ticking off transactions and being sure they were accurately recorded. It took British capital investment in growing American companies, and British auditing of those companies, to spark the initial expansion of American accounting beyond bookkeeping into auditing. Even then, however, as Ernest Reckitt of Chicago reminisced about his experiences in the early years of the profession, "cashiers and bookkeepers felt it was a reflection on their characters if an accountant was called in to make an audit, their belief being that public accountants were never engaged unless a defalcation has been discovered or suspected." In fact, writes Reckitt, "in every three new audits we would discover defalcations in every two," a condition probably due to the fact that each audit was the first, that there were no internal controls, and that the same person kept all the accounts.

It took the turbulence of a rapidly growing economy, pushing westward via railroad construction in the mid- to late-nineteenth century, to spur what Previts calls "new business and management skills, including the services of an emerging class of accountants and auditors." And it was this involvement in business that led to the development of accountants as full-fledged business advisors.

Emerging tax law also led to some interesting work. Among Reckitt's reminiscences is participating in a lawsuit that convinced the Treasury Department that obsolescence should be considered in calculating depreciation on buildings. The Income Tax Department claimed that where there was a ninety-nine-year ground lease, and the building on that ground could clearly stand for ninety-nine years, only 1 percent depreciation per year would be allowed. Reckitt convincingly demonstrated that profitable buildings could become unprofitable as newer buildings with better facilities became available, and that obsolescence should be acknowledged.

As the capitalist economy expanded, meanwhile, demands for corporate responsibility to shareholders were mounting, increasing the demand for independent auditors. We talk about the go-go years of the 1960's as a time of rapid business growth, but the turn of the century was a time of unbridled capitalism. It was a flamboyant era, with no holds barred, as improbable projects, unlikely of fruition, attracted investor dollars. When the projects failed, as they frequently did, investors had no protection. An instance involving Jay Gould provides a flagrant example. When he was accused of defrauding investors of some $60,000 he asked the investors to return their stock certificates so that he could verify their investment; when the certificates were returned, he destroyed them. Gould wasn't alone. It was an era of rascals. And it was an era that led to demands for accountability. Those demands were satisfied, in part, by newly formed accounting firms.

Many of the British chartered accountants who came to the United States in the late nineteenth century formed firms that were the forerunners of many of today's largest public accounting firms. Price Waterhouse, a London firm, sent its first representatives to the New World in 1890. Peat Marwick Mitchell & Co. looks back to James Marwick, a Scot who opened an office in Glasgow in 1887 and one in the U.S. in 1896. Pannell Kerr Forster traces its ancestry to Dublin and a man named Henry Brown in 1845; Brown's firm hired Scotsman Erroll Kerr in 1901 and Kerr opened for business in New York City in 1911. Other firms were native-born. Haskins & Sells, today Deloitte Haskins & Sells, was founded in 1895. Lybrand, Ross Bros. & Montgomery, today Coopers & Lybrand, was founded in 1898. Ernst & Ernst, today Ernst & Whinney, opened its doors in Cleveland in 1903.

Despite the rapid growth of industry and the associated need for accounting services in the 1880's, however, the profession was disorganized. There were no generally accepted accounting standards, there was little written to guide accountants in their work, there were no national organizations of accountants, and there was no legal recognition of the profession. Partly as a result of this disorganization, business users of accounting services often had little notion of what they were buying or what they could expect. Some businessmen characterized accountants as simply "expert calculators" who could rapidly and unerringly add long columns of figures in their heads. Others, perhaps ahead of their time, recognized that skilled accountants could provide expert business advice.

The Organized Accounting Profession

Disorganization began to turn to organization with the formation, in 1887, of the American Association of Public Accountants (AAPA). Earlier organizations, such as the Bookkeepers Beneficial Association of Philadelphia, were primarily local in nature; the AAPA was intended to be national. This predecessor to today's American Institute of Certified Public Accountants started out with just thirty-one members, thirty-one men who constituted almost the total number of accountants in the United States at that time. Even so, not all were in full professional practice. Many operated out of their back parlors and some, as James Anyon noted in his contemporaneous observations, could be found on street corners; neither practice contributed much to the professional standing of accountants.

But this was just the beginning. The newly formed organization began work almost immediately toward setting standards for accounting practice and toward instituting state licensing requirements. New York State passed the first CPA law, requiring licensing after successful completion of an examination, in 1896; other states followed suit. State societies were formed, beginning with New York (1896), Pennsylvania (1899), and Maryland (1900), and state boards of accountancy were established by legislatures to confer standards on the infant profession. Accountants were found across the country as the country itself grew, their activities mirroring the business interests of their respective locations. Many in Florida worked with railway companies (subject to Interstate Commerce Commission regulation, railways required audits well before other business enterprises), while those in Washington State relayed stories of arduous journeys to mines, logging camps, and salmon canneries.

State societies were feeling their oats at the turn of the century and, with a growing feeling that the AAPA was not a truly national organization (critics held that it represented New York to the exclusion of other areas), the Federation of Societies of Public Accountants was established in 1902; this Federation, with its mission of national representation accomplished, merged into AAPA in 1905.

Then, in 1913, the income tax became a national reality, ushering in another era of growth for the profession. Income tax laws became progressively more complicated—each new bill is often sardonically referred to as "the accountants and lawyers relief act"—culminating in the so-called simplification of the Tax Reform Act of 1986. It may be difficult to believe now, in an era when CPAs are so closely associated in the public mind with tax planning (sizable majorities in the Harris survey would turn to a CPA for income tax help instead of a tax lawyer), but for many years the American Bar Association charged the accounting profession with performing legal work without a license by getting involved in tax planning, tax preparation, and tax appeals. Lawyers considered income tax law to be strictly in their domain. It took forty years of discussion between the ABA and the AICPA, as well as several lawsuits, before this issue was finally resolved in the mid-1950's.

Income tax controversy notwithstanding, the accounting profession continued to grow. By 1916, when the AAPA changed its name to the American Institute of Accountants, it had over twelve hundred members (up from the thirty-one who got together in 1887) and, many believed, a mandate to represent American public accountants.

But things were not so simple. The name change itself was far more than a simple name change. As John L. Carey points out in his definitive work, *The Rise of the Accounting Profession,* this was a radical change. "The old Association had become virtually a federation of state societies, whose delegates had ultimate control of the organization. The new Institute was so far as possible modeled on the Institute of Chartered Accountants in England

and Wales—a national professional society, setting its own standards for admission, enforcing its own code of ethics, self-governing, independent of legislative influence, and dedicated to high standards.''

Dissension was not yet at an end, however, for two reasons: The new Institute appeared to be competing with the states in setting requirements for professional standing. And, although many still felt that certification was essential, the Institute continued to represent both public accountants and certified public accountants. In 1921, as a result, there was a split in the ranks of the AIA, and the American Society of CPAs was formed as a separate organization. It continued until 1936, when it merged with the AIA, under the AIA name. Combined membership, at that time, was about five thousand.

In 1933 and 1934, meanwhile, in the aftermath of the stock market crash of 1929 (and of continuing investment swindles marked by the lack of corporate accountability), the first federal Securities Acts were passed. These acts, requiring audits of the financial statements of public companies by independent certified public accountants, had a significant and long-lasting impact on the profession. Public companies must be audited each year. And many private companies, in search of financing, have their statements audited as well. While the Securities Acts created increased business for CPAs, they also created increased clout for the organized profession. The federal government required audits, but it shied away from providing auditors and even from setting audit standards, leaving both to the profession itself, as it continues to do today. From time to time, as in the congressional hearings of 1976 and 1985–1986, critics suggest that the government ought to take a more activist role. So far, however, the profession has been allowed to continue along the path of self-regulation.

Certification was required for membership as early as 1936, but it wasn't until 1957 that the American Institue of Accountants became the American Institute of Certified

Public Accountants. Today, although there are still non-certified accountants (primarily those working in industry and government, who do not perform audit functions), certification is widely regarded as a mark of professional standing. Even while the Institute was divided on the issue of certification, it was moving in that direction. Starting in 1917, the original Institute devoted its energies to the development of an examination, first used for admission to membership and subsequently adopted by state boards of accountancy as the Uniform CPA Examination. Satisfactory completion of this examination, designed by the AICPA and graded by the AICPA with the approval of the state boards, is now required in every state before the CPA designation is awarded. State regulations vary with respect to education and to experience, but the CPA exam itself is the same throughout the nation.

Today there are many specialized organizations of accountants. The National Association of Accountants, for example, founded in 1919, represents management accountants and financial managers. The American Woman's Society of Certified Public Accountants and the Association of Black CPA Firms represent their respective constituents. The National Conference of CPA Practitioners claims a membership of more than 1,000 small and mid-sized firms. There are groups representing internal auditors, financial executives, accounting educators, and more. But the AICPA is the largest group, representing more than 240,000 CPAs in 1986. As the largest organization, and as the organization recognized by the SEC in the areas of standard-setting and professional self-regulation, it is undeniably the voice of the profession.

That voice doesn't sing sweetly to every ear. Some say the Institute fails to represent the little guy. A study issued by the staff of the Senate Subcommittee on Reports, Accounting and Management of the Committee on Government Operations (the Metcalf Committee) back in 1976, for instance, claimed that the profession was dominated by the Institute and the Institute in turn was dominated by the Big Eight. Recent rumblings echo this sense. Eli Mason, founder of the National Conference of CPA Practitioners, asserts that "local practitioners have no power in the Institute."

The Big Eight do play an active role in AICPA affairs; as large firms, for one thing, they can afford to give personnel the time to participate in committees. But many small practitioners, as a look at committee rosters demonstrates, play an active role as well. And there has been a pattern of alternating the chairmanship of the Institute each year among small-, medium-, and large-firm practitioners. All chairmen are undoubtedly figureheads to some extent—they change yearly, while the professional staff remains in place—but the alternation does indicate a conscious effort to maintain equilibrium. In addition, as AICPA counsel Donald Schneeman points out, the continuing professional education programs offered by the Institute—largely unused by the large firms, which have their own extensive in-house programs—account for over 26 percent of the Institute's budget. As the Derieux Committee summed up its investigation of small and medium-sized firms, "AICPA has traditionally provided for smaller firms services which larger firms are able to provide for themselves." If the competitive pressures noted earlier continue, and succeed in polarizing the profession, AICPA may itself be polarized. For now, however, it appears to be meeting most of the diverse needs of its diverse membership.

It also continues to play a leading role in standard-setting and in self-regulation, both areas which determine the shape of the profession and, in turn, the shape of American business. In standard-setting, where the Securities and Exchange Commission defers to the profession as a matter of long practice, the profession sets the auditing and accounting guidelines that determine the bottom line for American business. Auditing standards are set by the Auditing Standards Board (ASB), an arm of the AICPA.

Accounting standards for financial reporting in the private sector are set by the Financial Accounting Standards Board (FASB), an independent body that has been in existence since 1973. Accounting standards for state and local governments are set by the Governmental Accounting Standards Board (GASB), established in 1984. GASB (this profession, like many, is chock-full of acronyms) is too new to be properly evaluated, but FASB has been accused of creating "standards overload," a condition in which there are simply too many standards to be read, absorbed, and followed. It has also been accused, in a seeming contradiction, of not responding rapidly enough to the need for new standards in emerging areas.

Self-regulation is the objective of Codes of Ethics promulgated by the AICPA and by the individual state societies. It has been implemented by disciplinary bodies sponsored by each of these institutions and by state boards of accountancy. The AICPA and the state societies, as membership organizations, have only the threat of withdrawal of membership to put practitioners into line; their preference, in any case, is for remedial action instead of punishment. The state boards can wield the threat of suspension of the license to practice, but rarely actually take such measures. Critics, as a result, claim that there is very little discipline imposed on wayward practitioners.

A vital element of self-regulation has been voluntary peer review, for firms choosing to join the Institute's Division for CPA Firms. Some critics charge that peer review is expensive, and therefore a burden for small firms to implement. But today, as congressional committees contemplate imposing government regulation on accountants, peer review appears inevitable. The AICPA has proposed its own mandatory peer review program, and is now supporting a similar SEC proposal. If this program is adopted, it will mean a marked change for the profession.

Where Are We Now?

The 1970's and the 1980's have been times of trauma for the accounting profession. On the one hand, increasingly complex business transactions and innovative financing ideas demand increased skill of CPAs. On the other hand, accountants are being held increasingly responsible for events that may be beyond their control. The combination is placing the profession in the glare of litigation and of congressional hearings.

Many members of the profession would like to go about their business without all this public attention. But perhaps controversy isn't all bad. "When Congress investigates a profession, that's an indication, perhaps, that the profession isn't doing a good job, but it's also an indication that the profession is pretty important," says Ed Kangas of Touche Ross. "In all these storm clouds, there's a great big silver lining because, as a result, I believe we will become even more important."

Controversial or not, it's clear that certified public accountants are playing an ever-more-vital role in the nation's economy. Let's take a look.

2

CPAs Today: Auditors, Tax Planners, Management Consultants, and More

"If any property is involved, divorce is a financial disillusionment more than a domestic separation," says Stanley Simon of Simon, Krowitz, Bolin & Hartman in Rockville, Maryland, a CPA who specializes in the relatively new and relatively narrow field of divorce litigation support. "Husbands frequently undervalue their assets, and we act as 'dollar detectives' to find their true worth. A successful determination in a divorce falls heavily on the shoulders of accountants."

What do certified public accountants do today? Let's put it another way: What *don't* they do? We caught a glimpse of the expanding role of CPAs in Chapter 1, but that was only a glimpse. Stanley Simon, quoted above, is just one of a rapidly increasing legion of CPAs carving out new and special areas of practice.

But the expansion of services is not without controversy. What services are appropriate for CPAs? Does continued expansion of services into new and untraditional areas threaten independence and objectivity? All the answers to these questions are not yet in, but a detailed look at the expanding scope of CPA services may provide some preliminary conclusions.

Three Basic Functions

Although industry accountants and those in public practice perform many of the same functions, there is one major difference: Accountants in public practice have the unique and vital task of rendering independent opinions on financial statements. This distinction is relatively recent. Until just over fifty years ago, as an AICPA Industry Committee position paper put it in 1982, "the traditional function of both internal accountants and public practitioners was to provide financial aids to help management meet company objectives. While public accountants had the additional societal role of evaluating the reliability of management's financial statements, the purpose and nature of this function was not well defined and was utilized by a relatively few large corporations. With the passage of the SEC Acts of 1933 and 1934, the profession and the business community focused on the public accountant's attest function and, because of this, the public practitioner's function and professional status has changed considerably over the past fifty years."

Many observers believe that the pace of this change is accelerating. The three primary functions of public accounting firms are audit, tax, and consulting. All three are expanding rapidly.

The *audit or attest function* is still the special province of certified public accountants; it is the only function, by virtue of licensing in almost every state, that CPAs and only CPAs can perform. But the traditional audit function, the rendering of independent opinion on financial statements which has constituted the bulk of large-firm practice for decades, is becoming a smaller part of the business for many firms, for two reasons: (1) Computerization has made auditing more efficient and less time-consuming; fewer hours mean lower revenues. (2) The field is inherently limited—there are few companies needing audits that aren't already getting audits. It may even be shrinking, as clients merge operations. Two corporations need two auditors; a merged corporation needs one. In order to expand, therefore, the audit function must meet market-driven needs. This is exactly what's happening.

Today, notes Robert K. Elliott, assistant to the chairman of Peat Marwick Mitchell & Co., three factors are fueling change: (1) Historical financial statements are not enough to fill the needs of people making investment decisions; they rely more and more on other information, such as forecasts and projections, which needs improved credibility. (2) The information economy has created tremendous new streams and sources of technologically generated information; "people are turning to us to clean up this information and make it usable." And, (3), the accounting profession needs growth to absorb people and create opportunities; CPAs are looking for new business and are eager to expand services to keep growth dynamic.

One way to expand audit services is to provide small business services. Many small accounting firms have always provided general advice to their small business clients; it's a natural extension of the accountant's role. The large firms are now beginning to go after this market as well via small business divisions. These divisions, designed to sweep entrepreneurial ventures into the accounting firm's client base, are often set up within the audit department. We'll look at small business divisions, even though they may be located within the audit department on a firm's organizational chart, as a part of management advisory services, to be addressed in more detail later in this chapter. The audit function itself, because it is both special and the subject of growing controversy, will be the subject of Chapter 6.

Tax services, both preparation and planning, are the second major accounting function. Some accountants were worried, when the 1986 Tax Reform Act was billed as a major simplification of the system, that work would diminish. With the law in its final complex and confusing form, business should be better than ever—at least for a year or two, until the new law is clearly understood. A survey of fifty New York City accounting firms conducted by Pension Consultants, Inc., in November 1986 revealed that fully 50 percent felt their clients would have to make completely new plans as a result of the new legislation; 48 percent—almost all of the rest—felt some revisions would be necessary. And a solid one-third of the surveyed CPAs believed that their overall business would increase as a result of the tax code.

Both companies and individuals need help in planning for taxes. What's more, individuals, especially highly paid individuals, are increasingly needing help with all aspects of personal financial planning.

CPAs have always provided this help; it's natural, as you help a client with tax planning, to help organize related aspects of the client's financial affairs. But today the structure of the help is being formalized in many firms in personal financial planning departments. For administrative convenience, these departments are often within the tax division. The transition is logical, says Stanley H. Breitbard of Price Waterhouse, especially now that tax reform will force clients to look at non–tax-oriented ways to save for college, make investments, and fund retirement.

Tax services have also expanded in other directions. As federal rates come down, notes William Gladstone, chairman of Arthur Young, state taxes become a high-cost area in taxation and a big item in corporate budgets: "There's a lot of money to be saved for our corporate clients." Valuation of properties, a subspecialty that is often administratively within the tax area because the original focus was to value for write-offs, is also a growing part of tax practice for many firms. Both tangible and intangible assets must be valued, as companies acquire other companies.

Consulting, the third major function, has seen perhaps the biggest expansion. Consulting isn't new. Historian Gary John Previts notes that what is now called "management consulting" was a typical function for public accountants in the 1920's, when auditing was a minor activity. Even so specific a function as computer consulting isn't really new; Arthur Andersen did what may have been the very first computer installation—a Univac system for General Electric in Lexington, Kentucky—in 1952. But consulting has certainly expanded. Both small firms and large are in on the act. As examples among smaller firms: Schneider & Shuster, a six-partner firm in Denver, acts as business consultants to their clients, emphasizing long-range forecasting and succession planning. Chicago-based Morrison & Morrison, a two-office firm, does extensive management advisory work including micro- and mini-computer installations, mergers, and acquisitions.

Computer design and installation is big business these days. "The next time you need help developing a big system," *Computer Decisions* magazine noted in July 1986, "a Big Eight accounting firm will probably offer it." In the offering, the Big Eight and their smaller colleagues are competing with non-CPA management consulting firms. The two groups are competing head-on, as they come closer and closer together, but there are still some differences in their approach. For the most part, says Simon Moughamian, Jr., managing partner of Management Information Consulting Services at Arthur Andersen, "management consulting firms stick to strategic planning; other firms do information planning, and still others focus on maintenance and operations. We're different. We provide one-stop shopping. That one-stop shopping includes project definition, identifying the client's needs and roughing out specs to solve the problem; creating, programming, testing, and training; and, finally, weaning the client to take over."

Specific expertise is addressed to a wide range of management information needs, from office automation to telecommunications. Clients may be in the private sector or in government. KMG Main Hurdman, for example, recently implemented a new payroll system for New York City, developed an automated accounting system to control finances for the Department of Health in the Commonwealth of Puerto Rico, and designed, developed, implemented, and installed a data processing system for Oklahoma's workers compensation program.

Critics of this extensive involvement, including organizations of computer consultants, claim that accounting firms should stick to accounting. Some go further and assert that providing management advisory services of any kind, including computer services, compromises auditors' independence. Heated arguments, as we shall see, can be generated about this issue.

A smaller subspecialty within consulting is litigation support. The largest firms all provide this service. But one of the outstanding practitioners in the nation, Marvin Stone of Denver, chooses to go solo. Each case is a challenge, ranging from testimony on the value of business interests in divorce, to testimony on corporate tax disputes, to testimony in antitrust hearings, to testimony in virtually any area where the interpretation of technical data is required.

On the antitrust front, for example, Stone has testified in several cases where competing newspapers have joined forces for business purposes; even though editorial functions remain separate, such mergers can be construed as eliminating competition. Under the federal Newspaper Preservation Act, however, such mergers are legal as long as one of the newspapers would otherwise have failed. Sometimes, though, the merger results in higher advertising rates, squeezing nearby suburban papers. These papers sometimes, even years later, bring suit. Stone has analyzed the data in such cases and provided litigation support.

A CPA can also quantify damages in tort actions. When a skier was killed in an avalanche, for instance, his heirs brought suit claiming substantial monetary damage, based on the victim's presumed lifelong earnings expectations and on the ski area's alleged negligence in not providing avalanche warnings. Stone, brought in to the case by the ski area, estimated the victim's probable lifelong earning capacity and was convincing enough so that damages were reduced by the court.

Industry Expertise

The division of CPA services into audit, tax, and consulting is a functional division based on technical expertise. There is also a logical division based on industry expertise. An auditor, a tax expert, or a management consultant may work with companies in a particular industry and develop special knowledge of that industry. The firm can then build on that special knowledge and extend its client base in that industry.

Denver-based Schneider & Shuster, for example, has its heaviest client base in the area of wholesale distribution, with real estate running a close second. In Sausalito, California, Russell Mustola feeds his own interest in music by concentrating on rock music groups. In Chicago, Morrison & Morrison is proficient in agriculture. "My father, who started this firm, was born in Wisconsin and had clients who were dairy farmers," says Art Morrison; this agricultural accounting and tax work led, down the road, to representation of foreign owners of American farmland, real estate, and business. Other local and regional firms specialize in auto dealerships or logging or building construction or whatever seems to fit the needs of the community and the interests of the partners.

Most national firms have many areas of industry expertise. Oppenheim, Appel, Dixon & Co., for instance, identifies the securities and commodities industry as a major client base. With clients ranging from broker/dealers to investment bankers, from foreign exchange dealers to arbitrageurs, the firm offers a variety of specialized services including portfolio management, system design and implementation, merger and acquisition consulting, and assistance in going public.

Laventhol & Horwath identifies one of its specialties as the leisure time industry of hotels, restaurants, and resorts. The original Horwath & Horwath started with restaurant cost control, which later expanded to hotels, managing partner George Bernstein notes; by the time the firm became Laventhol & Horwath in 1967, vertical integration of services had led to a high level of expertise in every dimension of food and lodging from market studies and financial projections on new facilities to redesigning a kitchen in an existing facility. "Our partners know how to go into the kitchen, know how a kitchen should be designed and how service personnel should be trained. Now we've expanded that expertise into front-of-the-house design. We'll help a new hotel pick its color scheme, furniture, lighting, etc." Mergers across professional lines expand this concept of vertical integration. L&H, for example, absorbed a firm involved in economic forecasting models; the models, which save on number-crunching, can be used in analyzing particular facility needs for particular locations.

Health care is another booming area, engaging the attention of many firms. With Medicare's prospective pricing system, designed to generate economic incentives for health care providers to cut costs, health care delivery systems have become increasingly competitive, leading to two major developments: (1) the growth of health maintenance organizations and other prepaid health plans; and (2) hospital insurance reimbursement schedules based on designated diagnoses rather than actual patient care. Both developments require a rethinking of cost-management systems. Deloitte Haskins & Sells is just one of many firms seeking to meet this need, with a health care industry program encompassing financial management, operations and productivity, information systems, and business planning.

One industry specialty often piggybacks on another, as

specialties expand in concentric circles. Pannell Kerr Forster describes two instances in which traditional firm specialties provide jumping-off points into other industries: Experience with hotel feasibility studies leads to assignments ("engagements," in professional jargon), and a new specialty, in office building and condominium feasibility studies. Expertise in hotels and health care leads to expertise in long-term care retirement centers.

Specialization

"Cocktail party chat always assumes 'CPA' equals 'taxes,' " complains Bill Weiskopf, director of audit in Arthur Young's Denver office. "I know nothing about taxes. I wish people would ask about my specialty, as they would ask a doctor."

Until relatively recently, CPAs, regardless of their level of technical or industry expertise, were all lumped together and defined solely as CPAs. That is exactly how many members of the profession would like to see matters stand. But just as medicine is no longer a single undifferentiated discipline, so accounting is no longer a uniform whole. And, just as the medical profession has subdivided into areas of specialization, so the accounting profession is subdividing as well. The process is not as far advanced in accounting, but it is under way.

The AICPA currently has three special member divisions: The Federal Tax Division, created in 1983; Management Advisory Services and Personal Financial Planning Divisions, both established in 1986. All three are voluntary membership divisions for AICPA members with an interest in the particular subject. The divisions were not established to monitor competency or provide accreditation.

Accreditation is a touchy issue, and one the Institute has been slow to address. Back in 1978, a Special Committee on Specialization (the Stevens Committee) completed three years of work and presented a report recommending accreditation of specialties. The report was accepted, then shelved by the Institute's governing body as it addressed more pressing matters. In 1986 the scenario was replayed, with a difference. When the Task Force on Specialization completed its work, making a similar recommendation, the report was both accepted and implemented by the AICPA Council. A committee on accrediting specializations was formed, headed by Merle Elliott, executive director of Smith Elliott Kearns & Company in Hagerstown, Maryland. The committee has started its work by addressing basic issues: What body of knowledge defines an area of specialization? How can that body of knowledge be identified so that practitioners can be examined for proficiency? What exams and procedures should be established to accredit a particular specialty? And, not least, what will it all cost? It's a slow process, says Elliott, because it takes time to develop a consensus.

Essentially, the committee on specialization is moving toward implementing the 1978 Stevens Committee report, with two changes. Where that report singled out two specialty areas (tax and management advisory services), the current committee is leaving a wide-open field; it will consider any specialty proposed to it (those proposed to date: personal financial planning and federal government auditing). And, where that report specifically excluded industry specialties, the current committee has not done so; "they may not develop as appropriate, because of the breadth of knowledge required," Elliott comments, "but we do not want to preclude them at the start."

So the national profession, as represented by AICPA, is moving toward accrediting specialties. Because the pace is slow, however, some states have chosen not to wait; this state action may even have precipitated the action by the Institute. Two states, in particular, have taken the lead. But their programs are very different.

The California Society of CPAs is not accrediting specialties but is offering in-depth study in the form of an organized curriculum. A personal financial planning program has been offered in California since early 1985 and will be offered nationally under AICPA auspices; a microcomputer consulting curriculum is under development. Each series of courses, as developed, will be offered nationally. "We believe a certification program, rather than accreditation, meets the need," says James R. Kurtz, executive director of the California Society. "We can phase new programs in quickly, then phase them out when they're no longer hot."

The Colorado Society of CPAs, on a different tack, has an accredited specialist program based on experience, education, and examination. Some fifty to sixty CPAs from all over the country—the program is not limited to Colorado residents—were accredited under Colorado's personal financial planning program by late 1986. "We decided not to wait, because the Institute moves entirely too slowly," says Lawrence G. Hupka, a Denver partner of Price Waterhouse who sits on the National Accreditation Board; the board, established under the wing of the Colorado Society, is expected to become truly national. Colorado currently accredits personal financial planning; plans are under way for tests in governmental auditing and computer systems.

Personal financial planning, first on the specialization menu on both the state and national level, is clearly of great interest. This isn't particularly surprising, since there's a growing recognition of the need for personal financial planning among Americans of virtually all income levels. CPAs recognize this need and see a market for their services, a market that can expand their client base. CPAs also see that they may be able to offer those clients a unique perspective. "Non-CPAs who practice financial planning may not be objective or otherwise well qualified," according to the 1986 proposal for an AICPA membership division for personal financial planning. "The non-CPAs frequently label their services as PFP while their true objective may be to market a product." CPAs, by contrast, are recognized and respected for "their objectivity, their integrity, their independence, their education and proven mastery, through successful completion of the CPA examination, of related analytical skills."

This very objectivity, however, can pose hurdles when it comes to implementing a financial plan. "Investment and insurance analyses are most alien to the CPA," says Jeff Saccacio, national director of Personal Financial Planning for KMG Main Hurdman. "We give our people specialized training; they must pass eight exams to be part of our PFP group." Despite this training, however, KMG people, like most CPAs, do not give investment advice; instead, they act as coordinator, working with the client's insurance adviser, banker, attorney, and investment adviser.

Not all firms take this approach, raising the issue as to whether CPAs who practice personal financial planning must register with the SEC as investment advisers. The AICPA Personal Financial Planning Division doesn't answer the question, but provides information to help members reach a conclusion based on their own practice. For CPA firms, in any case, a fee-based approach to financial planning is the only way to go. Commissions based on the sale of products, commonly accepted by non-CPA planners, are forbidden to CPAs by the Institute's code of ethics. This means that clients can count on objective advice, untainted by commercial considerations. It also means that CPA-generated financial plans tend to be expensive. KMG Main Hurdman notes that a complete plan starts at about $3,000. At Price Waterhouse, where personal financial planning is typically a corporate-paid perk for executives, a comprehensive plan could cost $5,000 and up.

These fees are representative for comprehensive plans prepared by national firms. But there are a variety of approaches to personal financial planning. With "segmented" planning, for example, a client will pay a smaller fee—perhaps a few hundred dollars—for a plan that provides an overview and then targets a specific need: caring for elderly parents, for example, or tax reduction. "Over time, topic by topic," says John Graves, director of technical information for AICPA, "the whole job will be done."

Despite the waffling about specialization, there is general agreement that all the areas of expertise discussed thus far—audit, tax, consulting, personal financial planning, computers, litigation support, and industry-based—are appropriate for certified public accountants. Some people may object to accountants as financial planners, some may oppose computer systems design, some may claim that any involvement in clients' business affairs may compromise independence, but, by and large, these endeavors seem to evolve out of traditional accounting and auditing functions. Other activities are not so clear-cut.

At least one firm, for instance, has an interior decorating subsidiary. Although Laventhol & Horwath's interest in this field evolves from its extensive management consulting services to the hotel and restaurant industries ("It's an additional service to an industry in which we are heavily involved," says L&H managing partner George Bernstein) some people, both inside and outside the profession, question whether interior design is an appropriate function for a public accounting firm.

Another major firm, active in retailing, has acquired a retail distribution and engineering consulting firm to support its own management consulting services. Touche Ross is proud that its consultants can work with clients to analyze and design distribution systems, facilities, and materials-handling equipment; implement store productivity services; and help improve sales and customer service. Critics suggest that certified public accountants have no business being involved, in any way, with something as specialized as materials handling.

Other firms provide executive search or recruitment services to their clients. What's more natural, they ask, than being requested to help find the right person to fill a management slot when they know management needs so well? Yet firms that are members of AICPA's SEC Practice Section cannot provide these services to SEC audit clients. Many CPAs agree that there is a potential conflict of interest. Even Charles Kaiser, Jr., managing partner of Pannell Kerr Forster, who relishes expanding services and who asserts that "profit is not a four-letter word," thinks that there must be some limits and that executive recruitment is one place to draw the line. "There's a conflict in objectivity," he points out, "in luring executives from one client to another. We won't touch executive recruiting, although we will screen candidates for clients."

Some firms define appropriate services in other, more pragmatic ways. "Our people thrive on dealing with very complex problems that have deep technical roots," notes Ed Kangas. "Executive recruiting does not offer that. We want both a deep technical base and a management orientation. Computer programming may be technically based, but it's not management-oriented, so we don't do it. We do design computer systems, however, because that involves major strategy. This is what's right for us."

Scope of Services

The scope of CPA services, as the above examples indicate, is generating heated argument within and outside the profession. The argument is not new. The Metcalf Report of December 1976 states:

> The most important requirement of independent auditors is that they be regarded by the public as truly independent from the interests of their clients. The "Big Eight" firms have seriously impaired their independence by becoming involved in the business affairs of their corporate clients. . . . The management advisory services provided by "Big Eight" firms are intended to aid corporate managements in operating their businesses, and necessarily involve "Big Eight"

firms in the business affairs of their clients. Such involvement creates a professional and financial interest by the independent auditor in a client's affairs which is inconsistent with the auditor's responsibility to remain independent in fact and in appearance. When a "Big Eight" firm recruits executives for a corporate client, shareholders and the public may wonder if the firm is retained as the client's independent auditor primarily because of the relationship existing between the firm and the influential executives it recruited. Similarly, the public may reasonably doubt the ability of a "Big Eight" firm to act as independent auditor for a corporate client which has also retained the firm to provide marketing analysis, financial management services, actuarial services, or other management advisory services. In such cases, an independent auditor not only becomes involved in the business affairs of its clients, but may be placed in the position of auditing its own work.

The Metcalf Report refers repeatedly to the Big Eight. In fact, as we have seen, public accounting firms of all sizes and shapes perform myriad consulting and business advisory services for their clients. The Big Eight, by virtue of their size, may provide a greater variety of such services. Smaller firms are more likely to focus on particular services. But it's a rare accounting firm, of any size, that sticks to a strict interpretation of its work in terms of accounting and auditing functions.

Management consulting itself is reaching further and further afield, with firms becoming involved in analyzing the impact of advertising campaigns, studying demographic market shifts, even developing "image" programs for clients. Amidst congressional concerns about whether such activities are appropriate, the Public Oversight Board, overseer of the AICPA SEC Practice Section, recently commissioned a survey to measure opinions about whether performance of such management advisory activities by CPAs for audit clients can impair auditor independence. Its results: Although no specific instance of impaired objectivity has ever been documented, the public perception is that advising or assisting management in certain areas could indeed reduce auditor independence. Performing plant-site location studies, designing or installing computer systems, or performing actuarial services for the company's pension plan pose no problem, according to the survey. But identifying merger and acquisition candidates, performing actuarial services directly affecting amounts on the balance sheet, or developing an executive compensation plan could be construed as impairing independence.

A number of observers see an inherent conflict of interest in accounting firms performing wide-ranging management advisory services. "The advice may lead to self-fulfilling prophecies," Robert Chatov, assistant professor of managerial and economic policy at the State University of New York, Buffalo, told *Computer Decisions* magazine. "When the consultant says, 'If you take this action, your profits will be so much,' there can be pressure on the accountant to make that prediction come true." And Abraham Briloff, Emanuel Saxe Professor of Accountancy at Baruch College in New York City, would prefer to see all management advisory services divested from firms that conduct audits of public companies, set up in a separate partnership.

In response, most large firms insist that there is a complete separation of audit and nonaudit responsibilities, that audit will always take priority (not only because it is the CPA's primary function but because, pragmatically, the assignment recurs each year), and that there is no conflict as long as they steer clear of actually making management decisions. Other firms, large and small, note that the client benefits when knowledge gained in one area (e.g., management advisory) is put to use in another (e.g., audit). Former SEC chief accountant John C. ("Sandy") Burton goes even further. "If the auditor is to perform his fundamental reporting function satisfactorily and marshals adequate talent to do this," he wrote in the *Journal of Accountancy,* "it would be a great economic waste if the auditor was not permitted to employ his insights to improve the efficiency and effectiveness of the client's operation as well as to comment on its reporting to outsiders. This does not make the accountant a manager but, rather, an adviser to management." In sharp contrast to Briloff, Burton goes on, "Accounting firms should undertake further integration of auditing and consulting services to emphasize the synergy which exists between them."

Should services, then, be limited? Concerned observers feel that expansion without limits may convert the profession into a commercial enterprise. But few, Chatov and Briloff notwithstanding, want to curtail *all* management services. Instead, the discussion centers around scope and magnitude of services. "Scope" refers to the type and variety of services offered; the question is whether specific kinds of services are in conflict with the independent auditor's role. "Magnitude" refers to the size of such services, and suggests that there is no conflict if nonaudit services are a relatively small proportion of the services offered. A subsidiary question is whether there is any threat to independence if nonaudit services are reserved for nonaudit clients. As might be expected, opinions differ all over the lot.

Coming down, on balance, in favor of almost limitless expansion, Robert Ellyson, managing partner of Coopers & Lybrand in Miami, doesn't think there should be any limit on services. "I think firms have expanded in appropriate areas," Ellyson says. "Artificial limitations or barriers are impossible to enforce and make no sense. Interior decorating has nothing to do with public accounting, and I don't know why a firm would want it, but it doesn't bother me that they offer the service."

Charles Kaiser—who says that "if you're profitable, you can be professional; you can afford to stand up for your principles"—speaks of the need for "reconceptualization," a theory developed by Theodore Levitt and written about in the *Harvard Business Review* some twenty-five years ago. "The railroads limited themselves by definition, by saying they were in the business of moving goods and people by rail; if they had said they were in the business of transportation, they could have grown with the times. Similarly, if we say we're in the business of auditing, we're taking a narrow view. We are actually in the business of solving business problems for our clients. Audit is part of that business." Kaiser goes on, "There's no contradiction between audit and consulting. Consulting adds to the ability to audit because the more you know about operations, the less likely you are to fall victim to management fraud. By trying to limit the expansion of services, we [the profession] are pointing a gun at our own feet." (Despite these remarks, it's worth remembering that Kaiser does set some limits; his firm, as noted, won't engage in executive recruiting.)

The necessity for change also underlies the thinking of Joseph E. Connor, chairman of Price Waterhouse. "When I entered the profession, the nature of what we were doing was to help companies do for themselves what they did not have in-house capability of doing. Today financial in-house capability matches the capability of the accounting profession in the sense of financial statement preparation. Had we stayed in our niche," Connor says, "our niche would have disappeared."

But perhaps George Bernstein, managing partner of Laventhol & Horwath, says it best: "It's exciting and interesting to discuss a variety of problems with a client. Restricting the scope of services diminishes that excitement. What's more, cutting out a whole segment of the profession will limit people, the people who are looking for challenge." Such limitation, by implication, will hurt the profession.

These arguments are persuasive. But so are the arguments of those on the opposite side of the fence. Past AICPA chairman Samuel A. Derieux, with the five-office Virginia firm of Derieux, Baker, Thompson & Whitt, thinks there ought to be a limit on services. "It's difficult to draw a line," he notes, "but if you go far afield from accounting expertise, you devalue the attest function. I don't like to see this happen." Along the same lines, but at just about the opposite end of the firm-size spectrum, Ray Groves, chairman of Ernst & Whinney, says that this Big Eight firm "intends to remain in the main line of professional services. We don't think actuarial, appraisal, and architectural services are appropriate for an accounting firm and we see plenty of opportunity in traditional areas. We're not opposed to new markets, but those markets should be ours and not other people's."

The arguments seem to come down to the need for independence in the attest function, the one function that is generally reserved to certified public accountants. "What makes us believable is our independence and our competence," says Robert Elliott of Peat Marwick. "But there's a whole gestalt; interaction with CPAs leads to the belief, or the lack of belief, that CPAs are credible. Belief can easily be dissipated by going into lines of activity that are inappropriate."

Both independence and objectivity are important attributes of certified public accountants, particularly in the attest function. Audits require total independence; the auditor must have no connection, no matter how remote, with the audit client. It's repeatedly noted, moreover, that not only independence but the *appearance* of independence is crucial. That's where Elliott's belief in credibility comes in. Objectivity, the requirement that there be no conflict of interest that would make the accountant less than objective in dealing with the best interests of clients, is a bit less demanding. Under the objectivity standard alone, management consulting and related services can clearly qualify.

Some services, however, as noted, raise observers' hackles. "I feel quite strongly," says Rholan E. Larson, chief executive partner of Larson, Allen, Weishair & Co. in

Minneapolis and a former chairman of the Institute's board of directors, "that as CPAs we have a franchise, a license, dealing with one aspect of services. That aspect is audit and review. I'm concerned that by performing other, unrelated services the profession may lose its identity. Even now the ads of the Big Eight frequently identify the firms as consultants, or don't say anything but the name of the firm; they don't say they're CPAs. I don't want us to lose our identity, to forget who we are."

An underlying fear, when it comes to limitless expansion, may be the specter of governmental regulation. B. Z. Lee of Seidman & Seidman in Houston, a former AICPA chairman, says, "The profession is changing and change is necessary, but we need to approach it with caution and there needs to be reasonable limitation on what services we should be providing as a profession. There's a perception by our critics, Congress for one, that we may be sacrificing our objectivity if not our independence. If we do not limit the scope of services, then someone will do it for us. Whether legislative or regulatory, such limitation would be more severe than any imposed by self-regulation."

Where self-regulation does come into play, at present, it's applied by individual firms to their own practices. The point at which most (but not all) firms draw the line is selling products. Even here there's a distinction. "I don't have any problem with selling software," Bob Ellyson says, "as long as that software is developed by the firm. I do have a problem if an accounting firm sells software developed by others. If I have an engagement to develop a system for a client, and sell someone else's software to that client as the best software, while I'm receiving a commission for selling that software, I'm clearly not objective; I have a conflict of interest." Some accounting firms, of course, don't find this objectionable. Some sell software and hardware. Some sell tax shelters, taking commissions and thereby violating the Institute's Code of Ethics. Some, it's suspected, are moving inexorably toward becoming full-service financial firms, offering any kind of product or service a client desires.

Individual opinion may differ, but the AICPA has none-theless attempted to address the issue on behalf of the profession. Back in the late 1970's, when the Division for Firms was formed by the Institute, the executive committee of the Division's SEC Practice Section (on which Rholan Larson served as a small-firm representative) tried to define what services would be proscribed for members. It was a difficult task, Larson recalls. In the end, five were designated as off-limits for SEC audit clients: psychological testing, public opinion polls, merger and acquisition assistance for a finder's fee, executive recruitment, and certain actuarial services. The focus on SEC audit clients is important. Many people feel that offering virtually any service is okay as long as there is a clear separation between audit and nonaudit clients, and they also see a difference between public and private companies. Independence, it's noted, is required only on audit engagements.

When the Anderson Committee was formed in 1983 to address the question of "restructuring professional standards to achieve professional excellence in a changing environment," it, too, spent a great deal of time on this question. "This was one of the most contentious issues," B. Z. Lee recalls, "we debated for a long time." The end result was a compromise between the free-market forces and those who would limit services based on their nature and their magnitude. The compromise holds that "nonattest services should not be limited by imposition of arbitrary restrictions. Rather, the acceptability of an activity must be determined by members in keeping with the spirit of the proposed Code [of Ethics]." The report goes on to say that members should, among other things, "determine whether, in their individual judgments, the nature or magnitude of other services provided to an audit client over time might create, or appear to create, conflicts of interest in the performance of the audit function for that client."

This deferral to individual judgment may strike some observers as wishy-washy. Briloff calls it "cynical and hypocritical. It will come down to 'How much fee is involved.' That will be the answer." But Lee sees the compromise as a positive step. "What is significant and the reason the hawks (including me) are happy on the compromise is that this is the first time that the Institute has said there is an issue and the profession ought to address the issue. Prior to this, the Institute took the position that there was no issue and nothing ought to be done—despite screaming in the halls of Congress and elsewhere."

There clearly is an issue. As the Anderson Report puts it, "Steady expansion into services not directly related to accounting and auditing has changed the profiles of many firms. . . . Yet those firms practice as CPA firms, and the public and other third parties continue to look upon them as engaged primarily in the practice of public accounting. . . . Public concerns about the independence of the CPA must be a paramount concern for the profession, and the issues arising from the growth of nonattest services must be dealt with. If they are not, demands could arise for drastic actions, such as divestiture of the nonattest functions or loss of licensing. The profession must act before such a situation comes to pass." The Anderson Report is a first step. But it remains to be seen just when and how the profession will act.

Perhaps public opinion will force the issue. The 1986 Harris survey asked a wide range of people (including owners of common stock, corporate executives, owners and managers of small businesses, etc.) whether they considered it appropriate for public accounting firms to be in particular services. Clear majorities of every group queried saw it as appropriate for CPA firms to offer the following services:

- Assisting in computer hardware selection and computer software design or selection
- Providing general management consulting

- Offering educational programs
- Providing actuarial services
- Maintaining service bureaus for various record-keeping functions.

When it came to appraisal services, opinion was split. This type of service was approved, over all, by a narrow margin, but top executives of medium and large corporations, creditors, and academics opposed the idea.

In two other areas, the results were mixed, but the weight of opinion seemed to be opposed to CPA firm participation:

- Executive search services were seen as inappropriate professional services for CPA firms by all those surveyed with the exception of executives of medium-size and large companies and members of corporate audit committees.
- Packaging and selling tax shelters, while seen as acceptable by slim pluralities of the public groups, was decisively opposed by "leadership" groups.

Summarizing its results, the Harris survey reinforces our earlier observations: "It is evident from these results that those publics most important to the accounting profession are convinced that CPAs should do more than audit. But they strongly suggest that there are distinct limits to the areas of potential operation. In turn, this means that there probably should be some orderly mechanism to determine what are the proper areas and what are not." It seems clear, as CPAs expand their activities to a virtual smorgasbord, that the issue of scope of services is unresolved.

3

Competing for Business: Marketing of Services

"When I was studying for my MBA in marketing," says Ruth Dumesic, "accounting majors laughed at marketing courses and marketing majors laughed at accounting courses. When I was offered a job at an accounting firm, I wasn't sure a marriage of the two would work." Today Dumesic, who is not a CPA, is marketing director for Williams, Young & Associates in Madison, Wisconsin. In 1981, when she started, Williams, Young was one of the first CPA firms in the country to hire an outside marketing director. It was a good move. The firm, which had a total of thirty in staff in 1981, had over seventy in 1986.

In the "good old days," barely a decade ago, accounting was perceived as a "gentleman's profession." Some CPAs look back nostalgically to a time when advertising and solicitation were contrary to the AICPA Code of Ethics, accounting services were more clearly defined than they seem to be today, and CPAs were more open with each other. Big firms, they recall, occasionally referred clients to smaller firms. A small-firm partner, if a problem surpassed his grasp, could freely call upon a big firm for help with little worry about client-snatching. CPAs from all kinds of firms, in fact, would openly share information.

But the good old days, if they ever really existed, are no more. Today competition is the name of the game, and advertising and marketing are essential elements. There is competition among firms of all sizes. And as CPA services have expanded, there is increasing competition between accounting firms and others (financial planners, management consultants, etc.) providing similar services. The competition takes several forms, some benign and some less so: marketing plans, advertising campaigns, uninvited solicitation, underbidding and "dumping" of services, and so on. Some observers view any and all competiton as terrible, a disgrace to the profession. Others see positive elements.

Positive or negative, it should be noted that intensified competition, in whatever form, is not entirely the profession's "fault." In the government's view, competition is a good thing. "Traditionally, lack of competition," the Metcalf Report stated in 1977, "creates problems concerning the price of goods and services, their quality, the terms upon which they are offered, and the development of improved goods and services that reduce the value of existing goods and services." Not long after the Metcalf Report was issued, whether or not it was directly related, the Justice Department insisted that the AICPA, like the American Bar Association and the American Medical Association and other professional associations, rescind its long-standing ban on advertising. Such bans, the FTC has held, act in restraint of trade and cannot be allowed. In 1978, accordingly, the Institute lifted its ban, paving the way for what some now see as cutthroat competition.

Even with the ban lifted, however, the Federal Trade Commission remains concerned about possible restraint of competition by other elements of the AICPA code. Deterring clients from changing accountants, or limiting the types of services that accountants may provide, the FTC Bureau of Competition said in a 1985 letter to the Institute, "may stifle competition among accountants and harm consumers without providing countervailing benefits." Some observers view these FTC pressures against opposing pressures from Congress. "Isn't it ironic," comments Ralph

E. Walters, director of professional conduct for the California Society of CPAs, "that one branch of our federal government has pressured us to abandon traditional ethical constraints as anticompetitive, while another branch of the same government tells us that competitive excesses cause loss of objectivity and independence, the hallmarks of our profession."

What Form Does "Marketing" Take?

"Increased competition for clients, greater consumer selectivity and the rapid changes taking place both within the profession and in business, government and society," marketing experts James G. Helgeson, Ph.D., and G. Eddy Birrer, CPA, Ph.D., wrote in the *Journal of Accountancy,* "have pointed up the necessity for firms to develop well-planned marketing practices that will give them an 'edge.' "

Yet "marketing" is defined in different ways. At Rubin, Brown, Gornstein & Company in Saint Louis—where I was referred to managing partner Mahlon Rubin as a "marketing expert"—the focus is on practice development and client relations. "We're not big on marketing as such," Rubin says, "but we do sponsor client newsletters and run client seminars and have been doing so for some fifteen or seventeen years. We see marketing as the concept of recognizing our present clients as the best source of growth. So we emphasize quality service and timely service and we ask our clients, on a regular basis, how we're doing." Similarly, the six-office firm of Crowe Chizek & Company, headquartered in South Bend, Indiana, doesn't do "a whole lot of advertising," according to managing partner Ronald Cohen, because "we don't see the benefit." Crowe Chizek, which recently hired its first marketing director, sticks mostly to public relations.

Public relations—and, for that matter, practice development—is often defined as community relations, community involvement. Sit on volunteer boards, be a Big Brother, run the hospital fund-raising drive, sponsor a Little League team, the theory goes, and you'll garner visibility. And visibility, at least in theory, leads to professional growth.

Sometimes such public relations efforts—what William J. Corbett, vice president–communications of the AICPA, calls "good-neighbor activities"—are haphazard, based on a vague notion that community participation is a good thing. Sometimes they are a conscious part of a marketing strategy. Conscious efforts encompass a wide range of one-shot and ongoing activity. Williams, Young & Associates, a one-office firm in Madison, Wisconsin, sent the whole firm out to volunteer in a fund-raising effort for local public television; staff was on TV from 6 P.M. to midnight one night in the station's annual auction. Magnuson, McHugh & Co. of Coeur d'Alene, Idaho, requires each person on staff to become involved in an ongoing way in at least two organizations of their choice—civic, recreational, religious, or professional. The firm feels so strongly about the value of referrals, according to *CPA Digest,* that it allows time off for these activities and pays any dues. Coopers & Lybrand, one of the Big Eight, with over five hundred offices worldwide, was the lead company in Summer Jobs '86, a project of the New York City Partnership that placed 36,239 low-income youngsters in summer jobs in the summer of 1986. This was a task that took many months of effort by many people.

For CPAs, public service, besides being good citizenship, is good business. It's a competitive gesture, a way to get new business. Practitioners can meet community leaders and generate client referrals. "People know our firm. We're up there among recognizable accounting firms," says Bob Israeloff of Long Island-based Israeloff, Trattner & Co. "It's a defensive approach. If our own clients see our name around, they feel secure in the decision to keep us. Clients like to be associated with a winner."

Participation in public service out of a conscious marketing strategy, however, is still relatively new. Many public accounting firms, reluctant to speak out about themselves and their capabilities, shy away from conscious marketing of any kind. Overt self-promotion somehow seems unprofessional to them. "Historically, the public accountant has always wanted low visibility," says Arthur Andersen's Tom Foster, in an article in *Outlook,* published by the California Society of Certified Public Accountants. It's a carryover from a long tradition of accountability and confidentiality. "You've also got to realize that marketing and public relations are 'soft' skills, relying on qualitative rather than quantitative methods," Foster points out. "That's a very different way of thinking for most CPAs, who are trained in being very objective and in quantifying everything."

Perhaps this traditionalist thinking lies behind the fact that relatively few firms have actually planned formal marketing strategies. A "disturbing number," according to an AICPA survey of smaller firms, report no strategic or long-range plan, no written marketing plan, no regular "needs-analysis" for clients, and no polling of clients for their perceptions of the firm's services. Many small and medium-size firms are spending money on marketing, in other words, but not necessarily spending it wisely.

The largest firms are in another category. The larger the firm, according to a survey released in November 1986, the more it uses mass media tools. The national and international firms reported substantially more use of publicity and advertising than smaller regional and local firms. For most small firms, as a report in *Accounting Office Management & Administration Report* in spring 1986 indicates, "advertising is a difficult expenditure to justify on a cost-benefit analysis." Fewer than 10 percent of the non-national firms, consequently, purchase paid advertising.

The big firms may take business away from smaller firms, but they go head to head with each other. Big Eight firm Arthur Young determined through market research, perhaps not surprisingly, that businesses find little if any difference among the goliaths of the accounting profession. To counter that image, and distinguish itself from the pack, Arthur Young has been running ads stressing its commitment to client service. " 'Taking business personally' is our theme," says Mort Meyerson, director of communications. One such ad, which the firm insists is based on fact, shows a partner delivering a much-needed business plan on Christmas Eve. (It's a far cry from 1945, when advertising was such a no-no that the Rhode Island Society of CPAs "resolved that CPAs should not use bold or black type in telephone directories.")

In another form of marketing, many firms, particularly the largest, produce a seemingly endless flood of publications. A Peat Marwick Mitchell & Co. history issued in 1982 notes the recent trend. "There are more than a dozen weekly, biweekly, monthly, and quarterly publications, including a variety of reports from the audit, tax, consulting, and private business departments, employee and practice development newsletters, an annual report, and some 250 brochures, booklets, and special reports. These cover a wide variety of topics ranging from banking in Papua or Macao to methods of calculating executive compensation or evaluating the investment performance of portfolio management. . . . The result of this emphasis on communications is to steadily reduce the mystique surrounding the profession and at the same time strengthen the understanding and appreciation of its role and talents within the firm and in the business and professional communities."

Many firms produce such information, although not necessarily on the Peat Marwick scale. Arthur Young goes a step further, with an ambitious book program geared to the bookstore trade. *The Arthur Young Tax Guide* has made the best-seller lists during the tax season for several years in a row. Although the book program itself is only a few years old, Meyerson points out, it's in a long tradition of "promoting what we know." Along the same lines, *The Price Waterhouse Guide to the New Tax Law* was one of the first in-depth looks at the 1986 Tax Reform Act available to the consumer.

Marketing Strategy

To spend marketing dollars well, whatever the size of the firm, means starting out with a well-defined marketing strategy. In this first step, a firm must decide what public it wants to reach: anyone and everyone? a specific industry grouping? a geographic focus? a financially-defined segment? The target public is related to the way the accounting firm sees itself. That means asking the fundamental question, Eric G. Flamholtz, a professor at UCLA's Graduate School of management and president of Management Systems Consulting Corporation, told an AICPA conference, "What business are we in?" Public accounting may be too broad an answer, in today's climate of specialization. "Are you in the health care accounting business? Are you in the high-technology accounting business?" Flamholtz asks. "It's going to make a major difference in terms of your competitive ability in developing a strategic plan."

Once these questions are answered and the strategy is established, the firm can decide what marketing route to take: publicity (speeches, seminars, published articles); promotional tools (brochures, newsletters, calendars with the firm name); advertising (either via direct mail or in print or broadcast media). Client newsletters are the most frequently used tool, by accounting firms of all sizes and shapes; some firms produce their own, while others rely on newsletters like the "CPA Client Bulletin" made available by AICPA. If a firm does nothing else, says Norman S. Rachlin of Rachlin & Cohen, Coral Gables, Florida, it should have a good print image, with a brochure and a newsletter, to get the message out.

More and more are beginning to understand the value of both nonpaid publicity and paid advertising. Israeloff, Trattner & Co., for one, is a firm believer in advertising. It runs one sports-oriented ad campaign for a general audience in a general newspaper, and another targeted campaign for its legal-support-services division in law journals. Its tracking efforts show that new business does indeed come from advertising.

If these tools are to be effective, however, they must be used in the context of a marketing strategy. And that means understanding what marketing is all about. "Marketing has to be client-centered," says Ruth Dumesic of Williams, Young, "not profession-centered. CPAs are used to telling clients what to do instead of listening to what they need."

Williams, Young started its marketing efforts back in 1981 by spending a year and a half on research. Before developing a business plan, the firm wanted to identify its strengths and weaknesses, see where they were vis-à-vis other firms. "We worked with a university to develop a survey, then surveyed five hundred CEOs by telephone," Dumesic says, "asking who their present accounting firm was, what they saw as the strengths and weaknesses of that firm, what they thought of the accounting profession, and what they wanted from their accountant. We found that our gut feeling about our lack of visibility was correct. Only three percent of the business community was aware of our firm. Some of our own clients didn't know the firm name, although they knew who worked on their account."

As a result of the survey, Williams, Young has been working on increasing its visibility to the business community. In addition to public relations efforts, including an annual Community Bankers Award of Excellence, given at the Independent Banking Association convention, the firm made a special effort to get to know local bankers and lawyers and get on their referral lists. Above all, Dumesic insists, "Every time we do something, whether it's sending out a bill or producing a brochure, it should be done with consistency so that the firm's image is the image we want to project.''

That consistency carries over within the firm, in the form of internal communications. A foundation for the marketing efforts, these internal communications include a correspondence manual, a speakers' list, a key-clients list together with a program for monitoring attention to these clients, and so on. While new clients are important—and Williams, Young, like other firms, maintains a prospect list—maintaining existing clients is an equally vital part of marketing. "We want to retain present clients, and to expand services to existing clients," says Norman Rachlin, "as well as getting new clients." One way to build services to existing clients is by what Rachlin calls "triangulation of services," being aware of the client, the client's business, the client's family, and the interrelationship of the three elements.

Some clients probably wish their CPAs would pay this much attention to them. But more and more CPAs are realizing that marketing is essential, that they can no longer sit back and wait for clients to come a-calling or assume that existing clients will stay put. Along with this awareness is a realization that client needs must be met. As Jay Almerico, marketing director of Wolf & Co. in Elmhurst, Illinois, points out, "We're changing from third-party service, based on IRS requirements or bank requirements, to two-party service based on client needs."

Almerico, like Dumesic, is a non-CPA marketing specialist. Not every firm can afford to hire a full-time specialist. Filling this gap, for many mid-sized firms, is one of several full-service associations of CPA firms. These associations—there are approximately ten providing a full range of services—offer educational programs, peer review, and, perhaps most important, shared resources. On the educational front, says John T. Schiffman of Smith, Batchelder & Rugg in Lebanon, New Hampshire, the associations have a distinct advantage. "At an Institute course," Schiffman points out, "I could be sitting next to a competitor. With another regional firm, by contrast, I can have a free exchange of ideas and information." That free exchange goes beyond the classroom. As an example, offered by Christopher W. Seidel, president of CPA Associates, Inc.: A member has a problem with a new software package. He calls association headquarters to ask about other firms using the same program. Within half an hour, he has the names of four other firms using the package, and the names of individual firm members to contact for help.

The associations, by combining the resources of many firms, enable those firms to compete with the large national firms. As *Accounting Office Management & Administration Report* put it in an in-depth look at associations, the "associations provide members, to some degree, the geographic reach, the professional depth, and the economies of scale of large national firms." Association membership may not bring a local firm up to the Big Eight in numbers, but it does help such firms compete with the second tier, the dozen or so firms just below the Big Eight in size. The National CPA Group, as an example, has thirty-seven firms in seventy-eight locations worldwide; with three hundred partners and two thousand staff, its literature notes, "If members were to practice as a single unit, the Group would constitute the twelfth largest accounting firm in the world."

Associations offer a number of tangible and intangible benefits. One of the tangible benefits is marketing. A small firm may not be able to justify the cost of a full-time marketing specialist. But if that firm belongs to an association with such a specialist on staff—Associated Regional Accounting Firms, for example, added such a specialist in 1985—it can share in the benefits.

Competition

Does marketing fuel competition? Or does competition spur marketing? It's a chicken-and-egg question without an answer, but it's a rare CPA who will ignore today's competitive climate.

It was possible for many smaller firms to ignore competition when that competition revolved mainly around audit clients. "Let the big firms fight with each another; it doesn't affect my business" was a typical reaction. Today things have changed. Large-firm ads that emphasize service to small businesses have aroused the ire of smaller accounting firms, whose traditional client base consists of small business. "They've expanded as far as they can with big business, and lost clients with the merger mania of the last few years," one small practitioner complains. "Now they're coming after our clients."

Indeed, most large firms now have small-business divisions (it's nothing new, Connor of Price Waterhouse insists, just a return to their roots as small business advisors) and are trying to bolster business among this market segment. They're aided in this effort by the frequent insistence of lending institutions that loan applicants, public companies or privately held, use a major accounting firm to audit their books. A local CPA may have worked with a small business for years, helping it build, then lose the client to the combined pressure of bank insistence and big-firm status.

This isn't new. "From the earliest days of the organized profession," John Carey writes in *The Rise of the Accounting Profession,* "tension existed between the large and the small accounting firms." But it may have intensified. The Metcalf Report noted, "As a by-product of the corporate merger movement that has concentrated control over the Nation's economic resources among fewer and fewer institutions and individuals, small and medium-sized

CPA firms have been displaced as independent auditors by the 'Big Eight' and other large accounting firms. . . . Displacement of small CPA firms by 'Big Eight' firms also occurs when companies 'go public' by selling their shares to the public. Underwriters and bankers often inform companies that a nationally known firm must be retained as independent auditor in order to sell securities to the public at the highest possible price, or obtain a necessary loan." In the last decade, with still more corporate mergers and acquisitions, there is still more firm displacement and, consequently, interfirm tension.

The AICPA believes the Division for CPA Firms, with its peer review program, can help small firms demonstrate the quality of their practice and, therefore, can be effective in helping them fight the displacement problem. But institutional ads about the availability of the peer review process have aroused complaints. Peer review is considered by many smaller practitioners to be expensive, although the Institute points to a rule of thumb for smaller firms of one dollar per day per CPA. In any case, those opposed argue, the Institute shouldn't promote one segment of its membership over another. The Institute, of course, is promoting peer review as a positive benefit for users of accounting services, and would like a mandatory quality-review program for all members. If mandatory quality review as proposed by the SEC is put into effect, perhaps ads like these will also be accepted as an image-building effort for all certified public accountants.

Some associations, as noted, have their own peer review programs—some of which predate AICPA efforts—and membership in an association helps some smaller firms compete with the big nationals. With a peer review system that ensures quality work, plus national and international representation, a local firm can call on another association member to pitch in and help when work is required for a client in another state or country. The associations typically restrict membership in a given area, to enhance cooperation. The operations manual of Associated Accounting Firms International, for instance, says, "In order to maximize candid exchange of ideas and information, it has always been felt that a geographic area should generally be represented by no more than one AAFI firm with rare exceptions."

Competiton, and the marketing efforts that feed competition, can be positive. "Competition isn't all bad," says Bill Gladstone of Arthur Young. "It's made auditors more efficient and brought down the cost of audit." And J. Michael Cook, chairman of Deloitte Haskins & Sells and 1986–87 chairman of AICPA, notes, "Competition, up to a point, has improved the profession, caused it to be more sensitive to client needs, more aware of the quality of our service. To use the Eastern Airlines phrase, 'We've had to earn our wings every day.' We can no longer take it for granted that just because we've had a client for X number of years that we're going to have that client the following year."

A sizable number of firms, however, don't see it this way. They see competition as degrading the profession. (Even Mike Cook admits that "the pendulum has swung a bit too far," with competition focusing on fees.) And they want nothing to do with overt competitive efforts. There are still a good number of firms that don't and won't have a public relations effort. There are still many that won't go in for paid advertising. A few will show the door to anyone who mentions marketing strategy. Even some that go along with the trend, seeing it as inevitable, have misgivings. Arthur Young may go in for image-building advertising campaigns, in an effort to stay abreast of its peers, but, as *Dun's Business Month* put it, "The partners still shake their heads in dismay over what they see as a creeping sleaze factor in accounting that allows solicitation of clients and markets an audit like a bushel of soybeans." And Donald Schneeman, AICPA counsel, notes that "rampant, cutthroat competition could well have an impact on the quality of services. It's already made CPAs who were professionals first and businessmen second into practitioners who are businessmen first and professionals second. And it's led to radical change. Mutual trust doesn't exist among CPAs the way it used to. And the sharing of knowledge is on the wane.''

Finding a Niche

There's a "polarization," says Howard Lutz of Schneider & Shuster, president of the Colorado Society of CPAs. "The big are getting bigger and the small firms are becoming more and more focused. These boutique firms specialize in a particular kind of business." The big firms, although they do everything, are characterized by their audit practice. The result: what Columbia's John Burton calls two separate and distinct professions.

With this division of labor, as big firm–small firm competition intensifies, some observers suspect that middle-sized firms may be squeezed out. Some mid-sized firms, in fact, wind up merging with larger firms. Some are taken over in regions where national firms seek expansion. Others seek mergers, perhaps because senior partners are nearing retirement or because those same senior partners want to relinquish administrative work to devote all of their time to practice. Despite large numbers of mergers, however, the AICPA reports growing numbers of mid-sized firms.

Many firms, both small and mid-sized, survive by finding a market niche. These firms can't compete with the big boys on large public company audits. Many don't even try. But review and compilation, tax, and business advisory services are up for grabs. Here's where it's important to pinpoint specific areas of service. The most successful new services, however, aren't offered in a hit-or-miss fashion. They aren't necessarily even offered on the basis of what a firm is capable of doing. "Sometimes we design services to fit our resources," says Jay Almerico. "We *should* analyze the marketplace and design services to fit client needs, recruiting additional staff and training them if necessary."

Services can be broad, or they can be specific. Crowe Chizek has one staff group dealing with management advisory services (from data processing to industrial engineering) and another group dealing with human resources management (from actuarial consulting to salary and benefit administration). Some specialty areas are specialized indeed. Stanley L. Simon of Simon, Krowitz, Bolin & Hartman in Rockville, Maryland, specializes in accounting problems related to divorce; Dupuis & Ryden in Flint, Michigan, has developed an expertise in franchising.

It's also important to pinpoint a target clientele. Rholan Larson notes, "Mid-size firms will have a hard time emulating the Big Eight unless they carve out a market niche, define a market for themselves." His firm, Larson, Allen, Weishair & Co. of Minneapolis, focuses on health care and banking, both regulated industries. "If you develop expertise in regulated industries, you can compete effectively, with this special expertise, with large firms. You can also be the dominant firm, as a generalist, in a community of under two hundred thousand. This is another type of market niche." Still another type is regional. Smith, Batchelder & Rugg, headquartered in New Hampshire, focuses its successful efforts on business in northern New England.

Underbidding

A major recurring complaint in the competitive wars concerns underbidding. It's not necessarily a new complaint. In 1933, Walter A. Musgrave, president of the Connecticut Society of CPAs, wrote, "We should guard against money-seeking and unethical practices, particularly with respect to *under-bidding*. I have a letter from a member who tells of a fee paid by one of the larger cities in the state for their annual audit which dropped from $1,000 to $350 because of this *reprehensible* practice."

The numbers may have changed—few municipal audits are conducted for $1,000, much less $350—but the practice continues. It continues in the municipal arena, where competitive bidding is the norm and where some firms seem to "shoot themselves in the foot" with ridiculously low bids. "We required rebidding on one-third of our contracts because the bids were so irresponsibly low," says Arlene Lurie of New York City's Human Resources Administration. "And this was after the GAO report, after the city controller and I told them at a pre-bidder's conference, 'We don't want cheap, we want quality.' " And it's probably intensified in the private sector since professional associations, such as the AICPA, have been forbidden to interfere in pricing. Today, small firms commonly accuse larger firms of using audits as a "loss leader" to win clients to whom they can sell other services. The feeling is that large firms, unlike small ones, can afford to sell services at a loss in order to get new clients and build relationships for across-the-board services. Discounting, in other words, may be consciously used as a marketing tool.

It's hard to document such claims, but the feeling is pervasive. Accountant after accountant in different parts of the country told me that other firms have come after their clients, waving the lure of lower fees. In Richmond, Virginia, for example, Sam Derieux of Derieux, Baker, Thompson & Whitt says, "We see firms using audit as a loss leader; it's disturbing." What's more, he continues, "when a larger firm engages in lowballing, it seems unfair, but when a firm of equal or smaller size engages in it, it doesn't seem to be very smart." In New Jersey, Ronald G. Weiner of Weiner & Company, comments, "The audit function is perceived as a commodity, and commodities always sell on price. The problem is discounting, as the largest firms become financial service supermarkets with very low profit margins." And, in Denver, David M. Dirks of Tanner, Dirks & Co., Inc. echoes, "Both big firms and small are underbidding. Engagements are 'bought' with significantly lower fees."

Is underbidding actually pervasive? Most complaints are general and unsubstantiated. But some are specific. Gerald Golub, managing partner of Goldstein, Golub, Kessler, a mid-sized New York City firm, gives an example: "We quoted $18,000 to $20,000 to one potential client for quarterly reports, an annual review, tax return, tax planning, and conferences. A Big Eight firm quoted $12,000 for the same work, fixed for two years. The client said we asked better questions; they would definitely hire us if the price were the same. What they don't understand is that the *work* won't be the same. The quote is inclusive, but a big firm doesn't understand what it is to meet the client for monthly breakfast meetings, to contact clients with questions, to return phone calls immediately."

Big firms don't necessarily like the practice, or engage in it, but they recognize that it exists. "The problem is lowballing," says Robert Ellyson, managing partner of Coopers & Lybrand in Miami. "We are being forced to compete on a price basis." "We see people lowballing in large engagements," says William Weiskopf, director of audit in Arthur Young's Denver office, "but you can't do it consistently and survive. The practice could lead to the accounting profession's becoming the next Frontier Airlines."

Big firms aren't necessarily always the culprits. Joe Puleo of the seven-person firm of Puleo & Stizbard in Hamden, Connecticut, acknowledges big-firm undercutting on price, then goes on to say, "There are always young sole practitioners leaving international firms (setting up their own businesses) who are so hungry for business they will take a job at any cost. Sometimes we feel we are getting it from both ends. But maybe that's just part of being in business."

Underbidding (if, indeed, the service is comparable) may seem to serve corporate needs by reducing costs. But this is a short-term benefit at best. Costs, inevitably, will go up. Moreover, auditors can do their best job when they know their clients' business. Knowing a business well takes time. A change of auditors means starting over. If pricing becomes the dominant element, cost-cutting may become the rule and the quality of audits may deteriorate. Businesses will suffer. And, in turn, where public companies are involved, the investing public may suffer.

Opinion-shopping

Businesses also change accountants for reasons other than fees. Sometimes they're dissatisfied with service. Fees are more often a factor among client switches from major firms; among non-national firms, according to a survey by *Public Accounting Report,* problems with service loom largest. Sometimes consolidation is the cause; when two corporations merge, only one corporate auditor will survive. And sometimes companies are seeking another, more favorable, opinion on their accounting practices. Companies may seek to avoid a qualified opinion by their auditors, and present what looks like a clean bill of health. Companies may want to "doctor" the books to cover up troublesome financial symptoms like excessive loan losses. This may have been the case with Beverly Hills Savings & Loan Association, which ran through three sets of auditors in the ninety days before federal regulators closed the doors in April 1985.

Opinion-shopping often stems from the fact that alternative accounting methods are acceptable under generally accepted accounting principles. In many areas, of course, accounting is as much an art as a science. Second opinions are often sought on complex transactions that can be legitimately interpreted in different ways. As a result, corporations sometimes seek second opinions to bolster earnings reports and create a more favorable impression. For one reason or another, *Public Accounting Report* reports that 542 firms changed accountants in 1985, an 82 percent increase from the 298 that switched in 1981.

Frequent switching of auditors, for whatever reason, sounds a discordant note in many ears. When opinion-shopping is the reason, both the SEC and the AICPA are alarmed. The SEC recognizes that corporations must be permitted to select, and to change, their own professional advisers. But it is also concerned that the process may permit dumping an accountant who adheres to his principles and refuses to give management the answer it wants when that answer is questionable.

The SEC monitors the situation by requiring disclosure of changes in accountants among publicly traded companies registered with the SEC. Since 1971, in addition to noting changes of auditors, public companies have been required to disclose any disagreement between management and auditors over audits of the two previous years. There's a feeling, however, that some corporate managements may be less than candid in their reports. Now the SEC is considering strengthening its reporting requirements, requiring firms that change accountants to reveal if they had "solicited opinions from other accountants on specific accounting issues concerning existing or contemplated transactions" or if they "engage an accountant expressing an opinion which is different from its former accountant's position." In another proposed change, the SEC would require disclosure of any issues on which a company has sought a second opinion, regardless of whether the company changed auditors.

Some think even these measures won't go far enough. Joe Connor, chairman of Price Waterhouse, would like to see punishment. "I believe that where there is a clear case of shopping identified, and wrong accounting is given in the second opinion, then the second accountant should be barred by the SEC from continuing an auditor relationship as successor accountant."

The AICPA, meanwhile, also concerned about the potential for abuses in opinion-shopping, has issued standards for CPAs who may be approached for a second opinion. Accountants who issue such opinions, oral or written, must consult with the company's current accountant to ascertain that all available facts relevant to forming a professional judgment are known and understood. Applying this requirement to oral comments should reduce off-the-cuff okays to alternative accounting procedures. But the FTC, always eager to encourage open competition, isn't sure any limitation should be placed on opinion-shopping. It wonders whether the Institute's requirement might deter clients from seeking second opinions, thus making it more difficult for clients to evaluate or compare accountants' work.

While different auditors, given the same basic facts, can legitimately reach different conclusions as to how to account for a specific transaction, both the SEC and the AICPA are concerned with a potential loss of public confidence generated by well-publicized shopping around. If opinion-shopping is allowed to continue unchecked, they fear, audits may become less trustworthy. And the investing public, once again, will suffer.

Non-CPA Partners

As a competitive move, in the expansion of CPA services, more and more firms are hiring non-CPAs to perform specific functions. Marketing directors, for example, are frequently not CPAs. Computer consultants, similarly, can design and install management information systems without benefit of a CPA license. Engineers and space planners, tax lawyers and actuaries need not be CPAs to fulfill important jobs in accounting firms. Some of these people, despite their lack of professional standing in accounting, become "partners" in public accounting firms. They're usually called "principals" (if only to satisfy state laws that typically require partners to be licensed CPAs) but, to all intents and purposes, they function as partners.

This is controversial in some quarters, where the prevailing view is that CPA firms should have only CPAs as partners. But it's a matter of course in others a non-issue. As long as non-CPAs don't conduct audits and render opinions on audits—the only function specifically limited to certified public accountants—there is no problem.

Problem or not, the practice of hiring specialists in various disciplines underscores the trend toward CPA firms becoming full financial service firms.

Contingent Fees

Remaining competitive in the marketplace occasionally entails a contingent fee arrangement: I'll do thus-and-such for you and take as my fee X percent of the money you save as the result of my work. A non-CPA management consulting firm, for example, might institute an up-to-date payroll system for a municipality, basing its fee on a percentage of payroll costs. Or a hospital, in another example, might offer a contingent fee to a consultant for a cost-reduction study. Under some circumstances some clients, such as municipalities, may be required by law or constrained by budgetary considerations to obtain some services on a contingent fee arrangement.

CPAs, according to the AICPA Code of Ethics, are forbidden from entering into this kind of arrangement. Under Rule 302 of the Code, professional services cannot be offered or rendered under a contingency fee arrangement or under an arrangement whereby no fee is charged unless a specified finding or result is attained. Under this rule, bidding for certain consulting jobs is left, by default, to non-CPA consulting firms. This does not please many CPA firms with consulting practices, who are competing head-on with management and computer consulting firms. In order to compete effectively, some of these firms want to offer—and apparently sometimes do—a contingent fee arrangement.

In order to deal with the problem, the Anderson Committee proposed a change in AICPA rules. Under new wording, the Code of Ethics would read: "A member who performs an engagement for a contingent fee would be considered to have lost independence with regard to that client because a common financial interest has been established." That loss of independence would mean that contingent fees are okay but—and it's a very important but—that the member would be forbidden to perform audit or review services for that client while the contingent fee arrangement was in force.

At its October 1986 meeting, the AICPA Council voted on a motion to submit this Anderson Committee proposal on contingency fees for a membership vote. After considerable discussion, sometimes heated, the proposal lost 98–97. While many Institute leaders spoke out in favor of the proposal, pointing out that its adoption might well forestall both administrative action by the Federal Trade Commission and lawsuits against the Institute, Council members, for the third time in five years, retained a ban on most contingency fees, with very limited exceptions. Some Council members believed that contingent fees are simply wrong. Some felt that the modification wouldn't ease FTC objections or solve the problem. And some were probably swayed by the results of a Harris survey, presented at the same meeting, which indicated overwhelming objection to contingent fees for audit clients and somewhat less overwhelming objection, but still objection, to contingent fees for nonaudit clients. (Interestingly, the only surveyed group favoring contingent fees were congressional aides.) As Lou Harris put it, "There is something about contingent fees that smacks of nonprofessionalism. You will be given credit for rejecting them, in the name of professionalism."

What happens now? It's very likely that the FTC will take action. Its Bureau of Competition has indicated quite clearly that banning contingent fees is considered anticompetitive and a restraint of trade, possibly resulting in fewer accounting services available to consumers. In fact, in an August 1986 letter, the FTC indicated that the proposed modification of the contingent fee rule "does not appear, on its face, to have eliminated our concern that competition has been unreasonably restricted."

Are contingent fees unprofessional? What about advertising? Are underbidding and opinion-shopping always a disgrace? Is rampant competition, in all its manifestations, the hallmark of an industry in transition rather than a dignified profession? Whatever the answer—and observers, both accountants and others, have different opinions—it seems likely that competition will continue unabated.

4

Onward and Upward: Education and Career Paths

"Black kids don't grow up knowing about CPAs. But it's a great profession. There's the satisfaction of the work, plus income and lifestyle and exposure to a world that is both broad and fascinating." This is Paula Cholmondeley speaking, member of the Board of Directors of the AICPA and senior vice-president and chief financial officer for Blue Cross of Greater Philadelphia. Enthusiastic about her chosen profession, Cholmondeley, who is black, would like to see more blacks, more women, more bright kids of all kinds, exposed to the world of accounting.

As competition intensifies in the accounting profession, accounting services are becoming both broader and more specialized. At the same time, in order to meet growing public expectations, the CPA must be both number-cruncher and management advisor, able to cope equally well with the minutiae of business and with long-range strategic planning.

Yet with all the changes in the profession itself, the path to becoming a CPA has not changed very much at all. Most aspiring CPAs still follow a four-year college education with a year or two of public accounting experience (depending on state requirements), then sit for the CPA exam. Beyond certification, if they remain in public accounting, CPAs in most states must meet annual requirements for continuing professional education.

Is this preparation adequate? Or are changes necessary, both at the undergraduate level and beyond, if accounting is to meet the challenges of the future? More to the point, perhaps, is accounting today, as an educational track and as a career, attracting the best and the brightest of available students? Are firms finding the kind of recruits they require to meet both today's needs and tomorrow's?

Beyond education is the issue of career progress. What does it take to succeed as a CPA? Is success measured only by making partner in a public accounting firm? And is success reserved for white males, in a classic old-boy network of a profession?

A profession's profile can be measured in terms of both education and upward mobility. How does accounting measure up?

Education

Accounting, once a popular major among business-oriented college students, has lost some of its luster. Many of today's better students, attracted by the glamor and salaries of Wall Street, are choosing finance and marketing instead of accounting. But there's still a healthy crop of accounting majors. Some use accounting courses as a stepping-stone, going on to enter law school or study for an MBA. That MBA may be in accounting or in taxation or in something else entirely. But accounting, as the only major profession that does not require postgraduate education, has also been a popular career choice in and of itself. Sometimes the choice is deliberate; sometimes it's almost accidental, but nonetheless successful. "When I graduated from Franklin and Marshall," says Charles Kaiser of Pannell Kerr Forster, "my uncle, my mentor, said, 'Do whatever you want, but first establish a career you can fall back on.' He suggested engineering, but I didn't have enough math; law, which would have required three more years; or accounting. I started in accounting and it stuck, although now, as managing partner, I consider myself a business executive and not an accountant.''

Few accountants will become managing partner of a public accounting firm. But most, whether or not they stay in public accounting at all, will find that they need to be business-oriented as well as numbers-oriented. Most will also find that a broad liberal arts education, as contrasted to a narrow vocational approach, will stand them in good stead. These changes, however, are slow to penetrate the schools that offer accounting degrees.

But talk of change—considerable talk—is in the air. And specific recommendations have been made both by the AICPA and the American Accounting Association (AAA). Back in 1978 the AICPA issued a report on Education Requirements for Entry Into the Accounting Profession. This report pointed to three essential segments of education for professional accounting: general education (with emphasis on communication, behavioral sciences, and economics); general business education (including more economics as well as business law, marketing, and finance); and accounting education (financial, managerial, taxes, auditing, and computer and information systems). This model curriculum is currently being revised, to strengthen both the technological and managerial aspects.

More recently, an AAA committee on the Future Structure, Content, and Scope of Accounting Education, chaired by Norton Bedford of the University of Illinois, issued a 1986 report asserting that "accounting education as it is currently approached requires major reorientation between now and the year 2000." A major shift would be from accounting as a narrow technical subject to accounting as broad-based economic decision-making. A second major shift would change accounting education from a four-year to a five-year program.

Neither recommendation is made lightly. The committee

points to significant contemporary changes in the accounting profession, changes documented throughout this book: expansion of services, increasingly complex standards, shifting public expectations. As a result, "a growing gap exists between what accountants do and what accounting educators teach."

Specifically, the Bedford report points out, accounting services are simultaneously becoming both broader and more specialized. As the traditional audit function declines as a proportion of public accounting services and revenues, firms move more and more into a wide range of other services: actuarial and appraisal, information systems, litigation support, financial planning, mergers and acquisitions, and so on. As CPAs have added new products and services the public, in turn, expects the CPA to have a "general manager's perspective . . . in addition to qualifying as a technical expert."

The same expansion is taking place outside the realm of public accounting. In government, the accountant has moved beyond auditing and into financial management; government accountants, as a result, need competence in systems analysis and assessment methods. In the corporate world, accountants who get ahead will be accountants who understand the goals of the organization and can work with senior management toward reaching those goals.

Public accounting, government accounting, industry accounting—all are undergoing change. But what about education? Despite some recent curriculum additions, primarily in computers and information systems, most observers believe that meaningful change has been far too slow. The committee noted, in fact, that "the basic content of most university accounting educational programs has remained relatively unchanged for many years and has not yet fully adapted to the changing scope of accounting practice."

What has happened, however, is that the need for more leaning, as technical knowledge proliferates, has led in some ways to less learning. "We cover more topics in each course," says Edwin Cohen, professor of accountancy at DePaul University School of Accountancy, "but we cover less depth in each of the topics. As a result, today's graduates are not as well equipped as their predecessors to step right into a job and start work immediately. They need more on-the-job training."

Some observers think this on-the-job training is entirely appropriate. They would prefer to see new recruits emerge from school with a broad liberal education, knowing how to think, and able to pick up and keep abreast of changing technical know-how. As Bob Elliott of Peat Marwick puts it, "Give me a smart person with a general education, and I can make him an accountant. Give me a person who knows debits and credits, and I can't make him smart and well-educated." Or, as the Bedford Report notes, many accounting educators question the current state of education on two counts: "They believe the material taught and learned is inadequate, and they question the effectiveness of traditional teaching and learning methods. These educators cite complaints that many accounting graduates do not know how to communicate, cannot reason logically, and have limited problem-solving ability as public evidence of the need to change university accounting educational processes in a fundamental way."

The Committee then makes some specific recommendations for change:

- The scope and content of accounting education should go well beyond technical skills to develop the skills of logical reasoning, a capacity for creative thinking and problem-solving, an appreciation of ethical standards and conduct, and a facility for effective communication and interpersonal relations. The aim: to prepare accountants for lifelong learning.
- Accounting education should build on a base of broad general education in the humanities, the arts, and the sciences.

- Professional accounting education should then include the design and use of information systems; decision-making and problem-solving; knowledge of the functional activities of business, government and not-for-profit organizations; financial information and public reporting; knowledge of the accounting profession's history, ethics and professional responsibilities.
- Specialized accounting education, which would be offered only on the graduate level, may then include taxation, information systems, auditing, and such other specialties—governmental accounting, for instance, or international accounting—as may be developed in the future.

There's considerable support for broadening undergraduate education, both in the academic community and among accounting firms. On the educational side, as an example, Dr. Jerome Kesselman, professor of accounting and law at the University of Denver, insists, "We've got to go broader. Graduates must know something about the technical aspects, but the computer is taking over the routine work of the auditor and the client needs broader help. The emphasis should be on analytical thinking, the logical processes leading to management decisions. We don't want accountants to be involved in decision-making, which compromises independence, but to know what questions to ask and how to help management understand alternatives and reach decisions. To do this, CPAs need to know finance, economics, personnel, sociology."

Bob Elliott of Peat Marwick concurs. "What we as CPAs are doing corresponds only dimly to what is being taught in the universities. We'd like teachers to train students to deal, not with just procedural matters, but with a more conceptual orientation so that the subject matter being audited would be irrelevant and the tools and technology of audit could be applied to a much broader range. The skills we use as both accountants and auditors," Elliott continues, "are more generic than you might think. Accounting in its narrow definition is measuring results of business transactions. Broadly, however, it is determining what kinds of measurements can be made, what principles should be applied, what system used to capture information, what internal controls will be used, how information can be summarized and presented—all applied to a much broader scene than financial statements."

But there's less support for other parts of the Bedford Report. The AICPA, for instance, while agreeing that a foundation in general education should precede education in professional accounting, disagrees with the rigid layering of the Bedford proposal. "Rather," says A. Tom Nelson, chairman of the Institute's Education Executive Committee, "students should be encouraged to continue taking non-business courses throughout their college careers. . . . It would be inappropriate to limit graduate education so as to preclude an appropriate mix of technical and non-technical subjects."

Perhaps even more important, the AICPA would like to see 150 hours of education (30 hours beyond the baccalaureate degree) required before candidates may sit for the CPA exam. Under the Bedford proposal, despite the fifth-year requirement, recipients of four-year degrees would still be permitted to take the CPA exam; the fifth year would provide certification in a specialty. In other words, according to James H. MacNeill, the Institute's late director of relations with educators, "This leaves us just where we started; that is, only four years of education would be required to become a CPA."

A Fifth Year?

The five-year program is controversial. AICPA has been supporting the concept since 1969 and vigorously promoting it since 1983, hoping that it would be adopted on a state-by-state basis (it's the individual states that set professional licensing standards). Even with the support of a number of other organizations—the National Association of State Boards of Accountancy (which has incorporated the concept in its 1984 Model Public Accountancy Bill), the Commission on Auditors' Responsibilities, the Federation of Schools of Accountancy—as of 1987 only Florida, Hawaii, and Utah required postbaccalaureate education, Tennessee had passed a law which is effective in 1993, and only a few other jurisdictions have taken even tentative steps toward that goal. The Institute's Anderson Committee, therefore, recommended that the Institute itself make five-year education (not an advanced degree, necessarily, but an additional thirty hours of education beyond the baccalaureate) a requirement for membership by the year 2000. "Such a commitment by the Institute," the Committee report said, "would send a forceful signal not only to the licensing bodies but also to the institutions of higher education concerned with developing acceptable education programs."

Some of those institutions may have reservations about the fifth-year requirement. In part, their reservations are practical: There simply aren't enough qualified people to teach advanced courses; there's a severe shortage of Ph.D.'s in accounting, as qualified people opt for the higher pay of public accounting and industry. The AICPA, in an attempt to build faculty members, recently established a financial aid program for entering doctoral candidates. It will take several years before results can be measured.

States pushing for the fifth year, meanwhile, have run into institutional opposition. In New York, where both the New York State Society of CPAs and the New York State Board for Public Accountancy backed a fifth-year requirement, it was rejected by the state. One of the reasons: "Baccalaureate institutions would be under immediate pressure to seek a change in mission at an increase in cost." Colorado got even closer. In the late 1970's the Colorado legislature actually passed a statute requiring a fifth year, providing a phase-in period before it took effect. But before the transitional period expired, another bill was passed eliminating the fifth year as a statutory requirement. According to Dr. Kesselman, who firmly supports the fifth-year idea, only two schools, the University of Denver and Colorado State University, were equipped at that time to provide the additional year. Other colleges and universities, without the budget or the staff to implement the program, fought the concept and won.

There are other problems. Some firms oppose the idea because they need people and want graduates faster. Bob Ellyson, past chairman of the AICPA Postbaccalaureate Education Requirement Committee, points out that in Florida, where the fifth year is now a requirement, "recruiters are urging students to leave after four years and pick up the rest piecemeal, at night." In addition, requiring higher education could have an impact on starting salaries. Those salaries are low as professions go, starting at about $20,000 for a recruit in most public accounting firms in 1986, perhaps a couple of thousand more for recruits in the Big Eight.

There may also be a human problem. Traditionally accounting has been a pathway into the middle class both for first-generation Americans and for first-generation college attendees. With a four-year educational requirement, it has been accessible as a profession, an "entry point for have-nots," as Bob Elliott puts it, and "piling up requirements sets impediments." Others agree. Dr. Cohen of DePaul says, "We do appeal more to lower-middle-class and maybe even lower-class kids who can achieve something in four years, a respectable job with respectable compensation and prestige. Making it strictly a graduate program would eliminate some of these students." A fifth year "will be a stumbling block for many disadvantaged students, particularly black students," adds Dr. Quiester Craig, dean of the School of Business and Economics at North Carolina Agricultural and Technological State University, the first black university to have its accounting program accredited. "It will be another gap or ditch they have to cross." (Countering this argument, Bert N. Mitchell, the first black president of the New York State Society of CPAs, points out that other professions, with substantially more demanding educational requirements, have greater black participation. "It is likely that more minorities with the strongest academic backgrounds would be attracted to our profession if it had a preparation requirement similar to that of medicine and law." Arguments to the contrary, Mitchell asserts, are arguments of convenience rather than concern.)

Graduate education, even now, is a clear road to the top. According to statistics compiled by AICPA, students with education beyond the baccalaureate level do much better on the CPA exam, have a better selection of job opportunities—30 percent of accounting graduates with bachelor's degrees were hired by public accounting firms in 1984–1985; 37 percent of those with master's degrees were hired—and receive starting salaries that are 10 to 20 percent higher. Not every graduate wants a job with a public accounting firm, of course, and other accounting jobs are harder to track, but the numbers are nonetheless indicative. Once employed in public accounting, recruits with higher education also seem to move further faster. A 1983 AICPA report cited one firm as noting that over a five-year period 36 percent of advanced-degree holders who were promoted to manager moved up within five years of hiring; only 20 percent of bachelor's-degree holders moved up as quickly. "Half of the partners admitted in the last couple of years have had graduate degrees," says Bob Ellyson, "but not half of the recruits."

Despite opposition in some quarters, graduate education for accountants may be an idea whose time, at last, has come. For one thing, some practitioners are sensitive about being the only profession that does not require graduate education. As Ellyson puts it, "You need more education in California to teach kindergarten than to be a CPA." For another thing, exploding knowledge has made it extremely difficult to educate aspiring accountants properly in just four years. And, for another, there is a feeling that the profession will tend to attract better students if the requirements are tougher; again, from Ellyson, "the best is attracted to the best."

Assuming that the profession does move toward a five-year educational path—and movement does seem inexorable, if slow—what form should that fifth year take? Some proponents point to the proliferation of technical knowledge, and expect the fifth year to provide a better technical grounding. Others prefer a broad-based general education. And some opt for a compromise, perhaps the first two years in liberal arts followed by three years of technical training.

Although the CPA examination is uniform around the country, every state sets its own licensing requirements. Both education and experience requirements, therefore, differ from place to place. The content of a fifth year will undoubtedly differ as well. But supporters seem to be united in the feeling that accountants need to be better thinkers, better communicators, with a better understanding of the world of business. Psychology courses might be of help in teaching accountants how to deal with other people. Specific practical education might be helpful as well. Not how to fill out a tax return, says Albert Ellentuck, national tax partner of Laventhol & Horwath, but "how to research a problem in an effective way, how to write to get ideas across, and a certain intellectual aggressiveness, the ability to keep after a problem until a solution is found."

In "Preparing for the 1990s: A Practitioner's Perspective," Duane C. Hansen of Arthur Andersen & Co., past president of the California Society of CPAs, outlined in very specific terms the capabilities his firm will look for. "In general," he said, "our recruiters will be seeking people with a higher level of business acumen and technical competence." Besides proficiency in accounting, entrants should demonstrate:

- Interpersonal and communicative skills, oral and written, including the abilities to negotiate and persuade;
- Analytical and quantitative ability;
- Broad-based understanding of business and its key functions—management, marketing, finance, etc., as well as accounting—together with a sense of the business environment and current business issues;
- An entrepreneurial perspective—in terms of both understanding the client and being entrepreneurial;
- Leadership and management skills;
- Computer proficiency and understanding of information technology and its applications.

A tall order—and one that is not currently being met. Whether or not colleges and universities can meet this mandate on the undergraduate or graduate level, CPAs clearly need lifelong education to keep up-to-date with a changing world. That need is met, in part, through continuing professional education (CPE).

Education on the Job

The big firms all provide intensive training for their professional staff. Pannell Kerr Forster, for example, puts out a twenty-seven-page catalog of CPE courses ranging from a new staff introductory program intended to bridge the gap between the university environment and the public accounting environment, to a partners' conference focusing on practice management; in between are specific-content courses in such areas as data processing, taxation, and the hospitality industry (a PKF specialty). Chicago-based Arthur Andersen & Co., until the recent merger of Peat Marwick Mitchell and KMG Main Hurdman the biggest of the Big Eight, spends over $100 million a year in educating its own people. AA's educational facility in St. Charles,

Illinois, where staff members come for courses lasting from one day to three weeks, handled thirty-five thousand students in 1985. The St. Charles training provides specific skills; it also transmits "the AA corporate culture," so that, says Dick Nerad, managing partner in Professional Education, "we put a consistent product in clients' offices."

Many firms are finding that explosive advances in technology, translated into new and innovative audit techniques, require classroom training for experienced professionals as well as for neophytes. Other training is required in changing tax law and new service areas. But not every firm can afford the expense of in-house training. State societies and the AICPA and the national associations of CPA firms fill the gap, offering a variety of continuing education courses. Some ninety thousand people attended AICPA-sponsored group-study programs during 1985, for example, most of them in three areas: preparing for the Tax Reform Act of 1986, personal financial planning, and federal governmental accounting and auditing.

Most states, but not all, currently require some form of continuing professional education for CPAs. Even in those states, however, requirements differ. If the Anderson Committee proposals are adopted, the AICPA will require at least 120 hours of qualified CPE courses every three years for every member. And that means every member. Right now, CPE is for the most part limited to CPAs in public practice. The Institute suggests that every member, including those in government, education and industry, can benefit by continual learning via courses appropriate to their interests. And as the number of Institute members outside of public practice grows, courses are being developed to meet their needs and interests.

Here, too, there are potential problems. Many CPAs in industry are skeptical of the proposed requirement. They don't see the need for CPE courses. "We need to keep current too," says Richard Piluso, director of internal audit for the Loews Corporation and current chairman of the AICPA Industry Committee, "yet right now courses don't reflect my needs, and I'm not optimistic about change." And they don't believe that their employers will necessarily either give them time off to attend or pay their way.

Courses and procedures may, in fact, need to be upgraded. "We must make sure practitioners, in public practice or not, are reasonably up to date," says Jerome Kesselman, who gives CPE courses all over the country, "but there's a problem with CPE as it's now implemented. There's almost an absence of adequate monitoring—of the quality of instruction, of the nature of the topic—and it's almost impossible to judge what participants are really getting." When people scramble to get into December classes, just to fulfill an annual CPE requirement, Dr. Kesselman feels, there may not be any real learning taking place. It's difficult to totally avoid this problem—human nature being what it is—but improved courses, required of every practitioner, should upgrade the quality of practice.

Beyond the Classroom

Education, even continuing education, is only the beginning. There are career choices to be made, both immediately following graduation and along the way.

Of those graduating with bachelor's degrees in 1985, according to an AICPA survey of sixty-one schools, 37 percent went into public accounting, 33 percent into business or industry, and 5 percent into government; the rest went to graduate school or to unknown destinations. Among those graduating with master's degrees in the same year, 67 percent went into public accounting, and just 17 percent to business or industry, while a negligible 2 percent went into government.

The first career choice, of course, is not necessarily the

last. Many accounting graduates go into public accounting initially, then move on to jobs in industry or government. Some intended to make the move all along, securing the public accounting experience only as a prerequisite for the CPA license. Some think they want to make a career in public accounting, then change their minds. And some make the move in reverse, gaining industry expertise and transferring that expertise to a public firm with clients in that field.

A few nontraditionalists sample all of accounting's multiple flavors. Arlene Lurie, for example, currently deputy administrator for Audit Services of New York City's Human Resources Administration, started out in public accounting. After three years as an auditor at Ernst & Ernst (now Ernst & Whinney), "when my husband and kids threatened to divorce me because I was never home," she moved to academia and taught financial accounting theory and auditing for three years at Brooklyn College. After toying with the idea of getting a Ph.D. in accounting and staying in academia, Lurie moved back to public accounting and became national director of Continuing Professional Education at S. D. Leidesdorf & Co. (later merged into Ernst & Whinney). The next move was to industry, first to Chemical Bank as an assistant vice-president in auditing and compliance and then to Barclay's as vice-president-deputy financial controller. "Then this [the government job] came up," she says, "and I was intrigued by contracting with a hundred CPA firms. I was right. There hasn't been a dull moment since I joined the public sector."

Others find a wealth of stimulating challenges in industry. Young accountants can choose career tracks in audit, in budgeting and strategic planning, in finance. They can devote themselves to specialties ranging from corporate taxation to statistical analysis. For those who have moved further afield, their problem-solving skills, intrinsic to accounting, have led to positions in marketing, operations, research and development, and so on. At the top of the business heap, quite a few certified public accountants are chief executive officers of businesses both large and small. Even more are chief financial officers, controllers, or treasurers.

Some start in industry and remain there all their working lives. Robert D. Thorne is an example. He started as a junior accountant in the controller's office of what is today USG Corporation just after getting out of military service in 1946. Today, after moving through the ranks for forty years, Thorne is vice-president and controller of USG.

A more typical route starts in public accounting, if only because most states currently require a year or two of experience in public accounting for CPA certification. (More and more states have so-called two-tier legislation, however, under which the CPA certificate may be secured without auditing experience but the individual who does so will not have a license to practice public accounting.) In Colorado, where there is a one-year public experience requirement, some leave as soon as the year is up. Five years, according to William H. Weiskopf, director of audit for Arthur Young's Denver office, is another turning point. Some leave public accounting still later when they find that they won't make partner. Some leave when they find the lengthy hours and frequent travel conflicting with desired lifestyle; this seems to be increasingly true, notes Weiskopf, among younger accountants. And some leave because they find a greater challenge in industry.

Dick Piluso is one who relishes the diversity of work in industry. "Right now I'm learning about ships and tankers, and what risks they take in a war zone," he said when we talked in late 1986, "because our company is starting a tanker operation, with tankers going up into the Persian Gulf." Piluso started his career with ten years at Haskins & Sells (now Deloitte Haskins & Sells) and left as a manager. "At this level," he notes, "you can see the negatives of a partner's work. It's very hard work, it's stressful, but it's not particularly challenging. What's more, once you have ten to thirteen years in public accounting, you're stuck, locked in to a career in public accounting because opportunities outside are very limited." So Piluso left before he got "locked in" and went to Amerada Hess, where he was assistant controller, and then to Loews, where he found his challenge in reestablishing the entire internal audit function. It's the management style he likes at Loews, where people "do what needs doing without regard to title."

There's plenty of challenge in public accounting, of course, and points of view do differ. Do these differing viewpoints lead to conflict between CPAs in industry and those in public practice? Yes, at least to some extent, says Piluso, at least in the auditing area. "Internal auditors at one time didn't relate well to external auditors. That's because the regimen of the internal auditor was not financially but operations oriented. This has changed a lot, but there's still some abrasiveness." No, says John Meinert, chairman of Hartmarx Corporation and recently president of the Illinois CPA Society. "There's no conflict between members in public practice and those in industry. In most ways, they have common goals. And they're working toward common objectives. Industry members, of course, can't be required to be independent; with first allegiance to their employers, they can hardly be expected to render opinions on their own work. But objectivity and integrity and technical know-how are required in both areas." Put another way, in the 1982 Industry Committee position paper, "With the exception of issuing an opinion on an audit, members in industry and members in public practice perform essentially the same functions for their employers/ clients."

Essentially, this is true. But it's also true that the AICPA felt it necessary to issue a position paper because many of its members in industry believed that they were second-class citizens, overlooked in the Institute's programs and policies. A key question addressed by the Industry Committee's strategic planning subcommittee, in fact, was, "Should AICPA represent all CPAs or only those in public practice?" The answer, after considerable study: "We believe the profession and AICPA can be strengthened by greater interaction between and equal professional status for the two major segments of the profession."

Considerable progress has been made within the Institute's organizational structure since the position paper was issued. Industry members participate in many Institute committees, and take part in the Institute's governing Council. With about 40 percent of AICPA's members in business and industry as of July 31, 1986, a percentage that is growing, perhaps it's only a matter of time before an industry member is elected chairman, a post that until now has been held only by public practitioners. But perhaps this would be too radical a change. To most people, within and outside the profession, the public practitioner is the very model of a modern CPA.

Despite the multiplicity of career options in industry, the epitome of high-status positions in accounting, in the eyes of many, is the position of partner in a major public accounting firm. This is the reward for years of endless hours for those who have stayed the course in public accounting. Not that the hours become less at the partner level. All along the way, CPAs in public accounting are expected to be on hand when clients need service. Coopers & Lybrand, for example, charts overtime among its audit staff and warns new recruits that staff accountants work an average of 175 hours of overtime each year, in-charge accountants an average of 260 overtime hours, and managers an average of 275. Those extra hours tend to be concentrated; in audit the peak months are January, February, and March. In other areas, and in other firms, overtime may be significantly greater.

What is the path to partner? At Friedman Alpren & Green, a medium-size New York City firm of about 100, the eight-to-ten-year progression moves from entry-level assistant to experienced assistant to "semi-senior," a position that involves handling significant areas within an audit, such as accounts receivable or inventory, and the preparation of complex tax returns. The next step is senior, supervising subordinates and working in systems installations and improvements as well as audit and tax, under the guidance of a manager and/or partner. From senior, the next move is to manager, the link between staff and partners. And the last move, for those who qualify, is to partner. As Friedman Alpren & Green's recruiting literature puts it, "Partners have the responsibility for significant decisions regarding firm matters. They maintain client relations, review completed reports and tax returns and negotiate and follow through on the collection of fees. . . . A partner is involved in practice development in order to attract new clients to the firm." Partners, of course, also have major responsibilities for overseeing and maintaining the quality of work.

At larger firms the path is similar, although advancing along the path may take longer. Pannell Kerr Forster, one of the fifteen largest firms in the country, with thirty-five offices, describes an eight- to twelve-year partnership route via assistant accountant, staff accountant, senior accountant, supervisor, and manager. Coopers and Lybrand describes an eleven-year pattern in the audit field, from staff accountant to in-charge accountant to manager and then to partner.

But how many people can actually make partner? Despite glossy recruiting brochures indicating that "there's plenty of room at the top," this may not actually be the case. Automation is altering the traditional pyramid structure of public accounting firms, with a vast array of junior-level people at the bottom and a select few at the top. Today, with computers to do much of the work, fewer recruits may be needed—although their work is likely to be more interesting. At the same time, there is increasing competition to get to the top. "There's general crowding, and it's more difficult to make partner these days," says the managing partner of a regional firm. "We lie when we say everyone of quality will make partner."

If this is the case and qualified people will indeed find it more difficult if not impossible to make partner, what will these people do? Public accounting has been, by and large, structured on an up-or-out philosophy much like that of the legal profession. Put in your apprenticeship, pay your dues, and make partner—or, if you don't make partner, leave the firm. "It's rare to find career managers," says Bob Ellyson. "It's too bad because people could stay, make a good living, have a challenging career. But there's a lot of pressure to leave, both peer pressure and pressure from firms who want the opening for people with partner potential."

This situation may be changing, although at a glacial pace. Some law firms, reluctant to lose qualified people, have created a "senior associate" position. And some accounting firms, in the same boat, have created senior professional positions. Arthur Young has taken another innovative step. After several years of consideration and discussion, and after hiring a personnel consultant to evaluate leadership roles, it has created a senior executive position called director. There's a subtle difference between the person who is a partner candidate and the person who is a director candidate, says Paul Ostling, national director of Human Resources at AY; it's a matter of "ownership perspective. Both partners and directors are expected to be proficient in a technical sense. But partners bring an entrepreneurial strategic contribution to the firm, leveraging their own contributions through interactions with others."

Creating a new job title, however, may not be sufficient. As a number of participants in a December 1986 AICPA Symposium on the Future pointed out, the basic structure of the firm must change if qualified people are to be induced to stay on in a nonpartner capacity. The firm culture must change so that partner status is not exalted. This may be hard to do, as Arthur Young realizes. Its first group of directors was named in October 1986 and, says Ostling, "It takes a long time to get in the culture and make it an esteemed position. It will probably take five to ten years to establish, but we felt we needed to start."

Not everyone is in agreement on discarding the traditional up-or-out philosophy. Some suggest that it may work in nontraditional areas. Keep the up-or-out approach in accounting, in other words, but drop it in technical areas where it's easier to have nonpartner specialists. Others suggest that the philosophy may apply to people who have already made partner. "Keep performance up," as one Big Eight partner puts it, "or the alternative is out."

Some partners may find it difficult to keep performance up. "Many partners have the wrong skills today," says John C. Burton of Columbia University. "They know accounting principles related to financial reporting but they are short on technology and business skills." As a result, he goes on, "A partnership in a major public accounting firm was once the equivalent of academic tenure, but this is no longer the case. 'Overtenured' partnerships are being forced to act to encourage the early retirement of partners before retirement age."

But there are staffing problems long before the partner level. In a highly competitive economy, industry headhunters are recruiting senior-level staff, CPAs with two to three years of experience, from public accounting firms. As illustration: Of half a dozen promising recruits handpicked at one national firm to feature in a recruitment brochure, only one was still with the firm two years later. Because retention is such a critical problem for all the firms, Frank G. Fusaro has been tracking statistics for the New York State Society of CPAs and developing campaign strategy that firms can use to stem the flow. The argument, which seems to be effective, is that while senior-level CPAs make a big salary jump if they move to industry, those who give public accounting a few more years and then move will not only do better in terms of salary but will move into a higher-level executive job. More important, perhaps, the studies have led to a general awareness of employee needs and, specifically, to higher compensation, better benefits, and less overtime. "The tide has really shifted in favor of the employee," says Fusaro.

That shifting tide, however, may not yet be visible to potential recruits. Not only are there fewer recruits overall but the quality may be lower. "We face a problem," says Bob Elliott. "The baby boom is through college so we're about to see an absolute reduction of graduates. At the same time, in an information economy, others want the same people we want." But the problem may be deeper still, rooted in perceived failure of the profession to change to meet changing needs. Dean Burton says, "What concerns me now about the profession is the fact that it no longer seems to be attracting the best and the brightest students. It worries me that in 1974, for example, eighteen percent of our graduates here at Columbia went into auditing and in 1986 less than one percent went into auditing. . . . Even at the undergraduate level, where accounting firms were generally able to hire their share of top graduates, there are signs that accounting is no longer the preferred career choice."

Burton, a former chief accountant at the SEC, sees several reasons for the entry-level crisis: Salaries are low when compared with such high-paying glamor fields as investment banking. More important, however, is a failure to challenge recruits. "The firms still largely follow a management philosophy of putting all new recruits together into a pool and letting the cream rise," Burton said in a 1985 lecture at the Brooklyn Law School. "Top students, particularly those with experience, expect to observe differentiated career paths." Moreover, while it's hard to prove, there seems to be a growing perception that public accounting is "no longer the best route to senior financial management or top management positions. . . . Thus not only do students see a career path with lower starting and final compensation in public accounting, but they see a reduced likelihood of upscale transfers at the middle stages of their career."

This may be a particularly dismal view—many observers still think of the CPA license as virtually a guarantee of first a job and then a stimulating career—but many practitioners do share Burton's concern about attracting top people to the accounting profession. Perhaps restructuring accounting education along the lines we've described will help, along with internal changes at firms. Perhaps entry-level people can be challenged in substantive ways; "we underutilize these bright people," says Ron Cohen of Crowe Chizek. Perhaps firms should think in terms of an inventory of skills, as futurist David Pearce Snyder told an AICPA Symposium on the Future, "get a coherent sense of the market and what kind of human resource mix is needed."

Meanwhile, despite the need to attract "the best and the brightest," both minorities and women encounter problems of their own.

Minority Recruitment

Approximately 118,200 of the AICPA's 240,000 members in 1986 were employed in public practice. Among these, representation by minority groups was appallingly small. Among the 100 firms with more than 25 AICPA members responding to a 1985 survey (the most recent figures available), with a total of 86,846 professionals, there were 1,966 Asian professionals, 1,221 Hispanics, 1,171 blacks, and 62 American Indians. This picture is, of course, incomplete. Minority-owned firms account for an additional 219 Asians, 151 Hispanics, 429 blacks, and 2

American Indians. In addition the survey did not count nonmembers of AICPA; no one knows exactly how many there are, but the number could be well over 100,000. It does not count smaller firms, which probably account for a larger proportion of minority employment. And it does not count the many members of minority groups employed in industry and government. But, according to a 1984 report by the U.S. Bureau of Labor Statistics, blacks make up just 5.5 percent of the accounting/auditing work force; this figure includes non-CPA employees, so the actual number of CPAs is even smaller. And Hispanics constitute just 2.9 percent.

But public accounting firms, particularly larger ones, represent the profession to the public. At the 100 large firms responding to the 1985 survey, with a total of 24 black partners overall— "a grain of pepper in a mountain of salt," says Sharon L. Donahue, manager of Minority Recruitment at AICPA—the profession is still overwhelmingly white. Deloitte Haskins & Sells alone has between 700 and 800 partners in the United States; it has 1 black partner.

It takes eight to twelve years to make partner, of course, and there haven't been many blacks in the pipeline for that long a period of time. Blacks also tend to go into industry. They don't see many role models in public accounting, either in firms or in their own families. And, notes Dr. Craig of North Carolina A&T, "public accounting does not offer as many opportunities in terms of economics. If all things were equal, our students who have the options— technical preparation and personal skills—would probably go with industry." Dr. Craig's assumption is borne out by the numbers. Of 16,155 accounting graduates from traditionally black colleges and universities from 1973 through 1984, 2,053 went directly into public accounting, 2,396 went into government, and 4,933 went into industry (the rest went to graduate school, worked for not-for-profit organizations, or had destinations unknown).

Others leave public accounting for industry later on. "I assumed I would stay in public accounting," says Paula Cholmondeley of Blue Cross of Greater Philadelphia, "but after two and a half years in public accounting, I got an interesting job offer and I've been in industry ever since." Sometimes the long hours and high-pressure atmosphere of public accounting make industry look attractive. Sometimes it's a subtle feeling of discrimination. "The problems minorities have today are in some ways harder to combat," says Cholmondeley; it's not necessarily overt discrimination, in other words, but "people promote people they feel comfortable with." As Donohue notes, "In public accounting, you don't stay with people all the time. You have different clients and a different set of supervisors on different jobs. And, if you have ten supervisors in two years, there's a good chance of hitting someone who simply won't believe you're capable. In industry, there's one reporting line."

Those who do stay with public accounting often go with minority-owned CPA firms. In today's climate, with Washington pulling back from equal opportunity commitments, Donohue notes that many black-owned firms have folded and others are scrambling to stay afloat. "For government audit contracts you used to have to show how many minority firms were brought in and for what percentage; that kind of requirement has gone by the wayside." It may have "gone by the wayside" as a federal requirement, but minority firms still compete for, and get, government and nonprofit contracts.

With attractive opportunities in private industry, in government, and with minority-owned firms, many blacks may simply choose not to stay with majority-owned public accounting firms. That's the impression of both Bert Mitchell, managing partner of black-owned Mitchell/Titus & Co., and Michael Cook, chairman of Big Eight firm Deloitte Haskins & Sells. Mitchell says, "Headhunters constantly have their hooks out; blacks get offers they can't refuse."

And Cook explains, "We have one black partner and that is not in any way related to any restrictions on upward mobility; our retention here is limited not by our willingness to retain, but by the opportunities that exist in the marketplace."

There may be even fewer black partners in the future at majority-owned firms because minority hiring, despite the sincere efforts of major firms, has actually declined in recent years. Minority recruits among public accounting firms peaked at 10 percent in 1977–78, according to AICPA surveys, but was down to 6.3 percent for 1984–85. "We're dealing with issues of the larger society," suggests Bert Mitchell, "and we see a pulling away from affirmative action programs." With this "pulling away," some observers feel, there's a change in the feeling that it's good business to hire minorities. What's more, the number of blacks enrolled in four-year colleges is declining, diminishing the pool of potential black accountants. Blacks make up 13 percent of the nation's eighteen- to twenty-four-year-old population, according to the Census Bureau, but only 9.2 percent of those enrolled in college. Perhaps it's not surprising that the number of blacks in accounting has not increased nearly as much as the overall growth of the profession.

But the profession isn't just sitting idly by, watching the numbers decline. The AICPA appointed its first Minority Recruitment and Equal Oportunity Committee in 1969; that committee continues to be active. The Institute also grants scholarships to minority-group students. Since 1971, when the scholarship program began, over $2,950,000 has been awarded to individual accounting majors; in 1986 alone, $335,150 went to some 450 students. And the AICPA sponsors annual week-long summer seminars for faculty from traditionally black and minority colleges. State societies also have special programs. The New York State Society, as one example, sponsors an annual "career day" to expose minority students to the accounting profession.

There are additional efforts by some firms as well. In 1965, Arthur Andersen & Co. was the first of the large public accounting firms to recruit at predominantly black universities. Since 1968 Peat Marwick Mitchell & Co. has placed special emphasis on the recruitment of both blacks and women. Touche Ross provides financial help to schools, and, says Ed Kangas, "We participate early, we help them with introductory programs for freshmen and sophomores, hold seminars, and so on."

Yet more remains to be done. Many people feel it's imperative to reach minorities while they are still in high school, to stimulate their interest in accounting as a major in college. Mitchell/Titus & Co. sends speakers to college campuses and to high schools, to encourage students to enter accounting. Bert Mitchell, in fact, introduced Paula Cholmondeley to public accounting when he came to Howard University to speak. Once students are in college, additional scholarship funds will help to keep them there. Award programs provide incentives. Summer internship programs provide both income and a valuable introduction to the world of accounting. And once the minority accountant is on the job, it helps if firms provide guidance in career development and client relationships.

Special efforts may be necessary. After all, as Cholmondeley says, "If other professions are more effective at recruiting the best and the brightest, regardless of race, we lock ourselves out of a large segment of the population."

Women in Accounting

There's no shortage of numbers when it comes to women. Since male/female data on accounting graduates were first collected by the AICPA, the percentage of female graduates rose from 28 percent in 1976–77 to 48 percent in 1984–85. New recruits hired by public accounting firms in

1984–85, both those with bachelor's degrees and those with master's degrees, were 57 percent male and 43 percent female. By now, many firms are reporting new hires at about 50–50.

But getting started and moving ahead are two different things. Although women are at least as technically competent as men—there is no disagreement on this score—they still seem to face hurdles when it comes to advancement. A 1985 statistical survey of 12,000 women CPAs by the American Woman's Society of Certified Public Accountants showed that just 1.9 percent of the respondents were partners in international and national firms; 9.4 percent were partners in local firms. Again, women are relatively new to the profession and it may be a hopeful sign that 20.6 percent are managers and 28.1 percent are supervisors. Presumably, these women are on the road to partnership.

They won't all make partner, of course. Some may not be qualified. Some will leave for industry before they find out if they're qualified. And some will be blocked by prejudice. Women in accounting today seem to face practical problems, outright discrimination, and, most often, a form of subtle, unspoken discrimination.

On the practical front, women in accounting face the same problems as women in any hard-driving profession: How do you mesh marriage, especially marriage with motherhood, and a career? Many women feel they have to make choices. "I can't function as a senior executive and also be somebody's mother," says Paula Cholmondeley. Other women don't feel they should be compelled to make such choices. They may not expect their firms to provide day care centers, but they do hope for understanding of family responsibilities, especially when babies are newly born. Once this initial time crunch is past, women seem to function well; given sufficient notice most take on just as much travel and responsibility as men. Sufficient notice, however, may be crucial. "The biggest issue is not daily care," says Brenda Acken, secretary/treasurer of South Atlantic Coal Company in Bluefield, West Virginia, and chairman of the AICPA's Upward Mobility of Women Special Committee, "but what happens when there is an unexpected dinner with a client, travel, or work on Saturday."

Another practical problem, one that seems to affect women more than men, is transfer of a spouse. When Crowe Chizek & Co., a six-office regional firm in the Midwest, sought reasons for the high turnover among its female staff, it found that the largest number of departures, including some women who were close to making partner, were for just one reason: their husbands were transferred to another city. Ronald Cohen, the firm's managing partner, finds this a frustrating problem, one without an apparent solution.

Still, practical problems, no matter how frustrating, can often be solved if enough time and thought are devoted to finding a solution. But what do you do about outright discrimination, other than bringing the force of the law to bear? That's what Ann Hopkins did when she sued Price Waterhouse in 1985—and won—because the firm refused to promote her to partner. The United States District Court for the District of Columbia found that firms may use subjective criteria for evaluating potential partners, but that they may not include sterotyped assumptions about women in those subjective criteria. This case follows a Supreme Court 1984 ruling, in *Hishon* v. *King & Spalding* (a law firm), that promotion to partnership is subject to Title VII of the Civil Rights Act of 1964 and cannot be based on consideration of sex.

Outright discrimination in this enlightened era is probably relatively rare. It's certainly difficult to prove. Hopkins was able to document, to the court's satisfaction, a repeated pattern of stereotyping. Far more frequent, however, is a pattern of subtle discrimination and insensitivity. "Child care and flex-time are not the issues," says Brenda

Acken, "but attitude." There appears to be an "old-boy network" that keeps women out of management ranks in virtually every field. More than half of the respondents to a 1985 *Harvard Business Review* survey don't think women will ever be accepted wholly in business. Acceptance is easier at the entry level, however, and fades as women move upward. Women weren't accepted at any level in accounting twenty years ago. Today, at the entry level, all is well. "In initial hiring, and in the first two or three levels of management, doors are open and women are fully accepted," according to Acken. "But five or more years into the profession, women begin to notice a pattern of subtle discrimination."

The big stumbling block seems to be practice development. Women are viewed as less capable when it comes to lining up clients or, as one woman told *CPA Digest* for its 1986 roundup on the "velvet ghetto," "Women are seen as having limited potential because they can't take part in the friendly golf games where male mentoring takes place." Some people, however, claim that this just isn't so. "Five years ago we were wrestling with the fact that the women, as they approach partnership, were not nearly as effective in generating new clients for the firm," says Ed Kangas. "Today we find that our young women are equally capable of generating new clients as the men are, and when they are able to do that, they get admitted to the partnership. The average age of women coming into the partnership is now identical to the average age of men coming into the partnership." Some people say it never was a problem. "I do not subscribe to the theory that women have difficulty with practice development," says Pete Scanlon, chairman of Coopers & Lybrand. "In 1986 we admitted twelve women partners out of a total of sixty-eight; overall we're approaching 10 percent. Both the absolute numbers and the percentage are growing each year, and with a relatively short history of women in the profession."

It may all depend on where you sit. But there may also

be a feeling on the part of male partners that their clients won't take kindly to female partners running a job. In part this may be true. Audit clients always interview "to be sure that we have the right chemistry between the auditor and the auditee," says Robert Thorne of USG. "I'm not sure that we would be ready for a female partner." When management isn't ready, or the firm doesn't think it is, then the auditor doesn't assign a female partner. But, Thorne continues, "Maybe they [the firms] ought to be a little more aggressive in that respect." Clients might shape up, in other words, if firms led the way.

Although many accountants believe, as the AICPA Future Issues Committee put it, that upward mobility within the profession, particularly admission to partnership, is more difficult for women than for men, the issue is being addressed. One firm, for example, has a "reduced load" program for new parents; participants work fewer hours with the understanding that it will take longer to rise within the organization. As Michael Cook puts it, "We just have to be a little creative, with flexible work scheduling and things of this type. It would be a terrible mistake for us to employ 50 percent women, to expect that in the normal cycle 50 percent of our partners will be women over a period of time, and not to recognize whatever unique circumstances they may have."

Some smaller firms, although they won't be quoted, duck the problem by refusing to hire new women graduates. One three-office firm, after finding that 80 percent of the women it hired left within four years, told its campus recruiters "no women." This firm, however, is willing to consider older women, whom it considers more stable.

Other firms realize that they must address the issue in a comprehensive way. Arthur Young, concerned about rising turnover, has a task force trying to determine the causes. Although it's difficult to gather information—some people deny that there's any problem at all, and many women fear that they risk their careers by saying too much—the task force expects to be able to make some specific recommendations. At Crowe Chizek, when turnover rate among entry-level people reached unacceptable levels, a committee was formed to examine the impact of women on the firm. The committee made several specific recommendations:

- Courses should be designed to assist women's integration into the firm; these courses should focus not on technical skills but on improving managerial techniques and overall business ability.
- Entry-level people need role models, and the visibility of women at the top should be increased. Women should be included in recruiting teams, involved in public relations efforts representing the firm, teach in-house continuing education courses, and take part in presentations to clients.
- Maternity leave policies were reviewed and standardized so that women can leave, have their children, make an adjustment, and come back, all without being viewed as a special situation.
- In an effort to reduce turnover, the firm will look to somewhat older women with stabilized family lives; these new hires will be returning to work after raising their families.
- Although the firm is maintaining its up-or-out policy, it is willing to consider a slower partnership track.

All of this is relatively new and, as Ron Cohen points out, it's too soon to know if it will work. "But we think we've sensitized the staff. There used to be a lot of joking by males about the career commitment of females. We hope there's less of this now."

Sensitizing is also what the AICPA Committee on Upward Mobility of Women is all about. It has held several meetings, exploring subjective impressions of both men and women about the role of women in accounting. A new AICPA task force on women in accounting will explore the problem from the firms' point of view. At the same time a number of state societies are taking action; half a dozen, in a 1986 survey, reported a task force or committee studying the role of women in the profession.

Intelligent people realize that this isn't solely a "woman's problem." With one-third of all new businesses started by women, it makes hardheaded business sense to nurture women CPAs. Most firms, along with most of the profession's leaders, recognize this fact.

5

Rules of the Road: Standards and Codes

"It's a complex business world. Pensions are complex, leasing is complex, financial institutions and new instruments are very complex," says J. Michael Cook, chairman of both Deloitte Haskins & Sells and the AICPA. "To suggest that you use your good old auditor's judgment and go in there and logic will prevail, in the complex environment we're in, is simply not realistic. We do need standards."

Accounting, of necessity, is a game played by rules. The rules change from time to time and, even when seemingly fixed, may be interpreted differently by different players. But the rules do lend structure and discipline to the practice of accounting. The rule-making process, therefore, is worth examining.

Auditing standards are set by the Auditing Standards Board, an arm of the AICPA. But auditing, in which financial records are examined, is the second step. Accounting, by which financial records are prepared and financial statements compiled, comes first. Yet, as John L. Carey points out in *The Rise of the Accounting Profession,* the setting of accounting standards has been a far more tumultuous process than the setting of auditing standards. "One reason for this, no doubt, is that the extent and adequacy of their examinations are the responsibility of the accountants alone, whereas management, auditors, and regulatory bodies have shared responsibility for the representations made in financial statements. In the development of accounting principles, therefore, management, the stock exchanges, and the SEC, as well as the accounting profession, have had an influential voice.''

All of these parties still play important, sometimes conflicting roles. Management wants to put the best possible face on things, coming up with a profitable bottom line, while the stock exchanges and the SEC want comparability of information and investor protection. Management, in particular, has a lot to say about which accounting principles are used to prepare financial statements; that's why auditors' opinions always implicitly indicate that the financial statements are the representation of management, which has primary responsibility for them.

There is room for legitimate difference of opinion about allocating certain revenues and expenses. There is also room for borderline practices. In the summer of 1986, as illustration, *Barron's* had a lengthy article on business practices in the funeral industry. It has long been customary to sell cemetery lots well ahead of need; in a relatively new practice, interment services are sold on the same basis. Both the plot and the services are generally paid for on the installment plan, with considerable attrition among customers along the way. But one company records such sales as revenue as soon as the customer signs on the dotted line. Its major competitor, by contrast, follows accounting practices used in the real estate industry and records sales only after about 20 percent of the installment payments are received.

Questions can be raised about both companies' practices. How, for example, do you predict costs to meet a contractual obligation at an indeterminate time in the future? Disregarding such questions and their impact on the bottom line, adherence to generally accepted accounting principles, if those principles were completely codified, would forestall this kind of intra-industry disparity in recording revenues. Investors, as a result, might be able to make valid comparisons of the financial statements of competing companies. But generally accepted accounting principles, despite considerable progress toward codification, still permit a lot of leeway. As *Fortune* magazine said in 1960, "It is a truism in the profession, though it still seems a bit shocking to many businessmen, that two different accountants in possession of the same figures may construct two considerably dissimilar balance sheets." There is still a kernel of truth in this statement, although there's also no denying that we've come a long way toward comparability since 1960.

In the beginning, after the passage of the first securities legislation in the 1930's, there were very few rules. When the SEC deferred to the accounting profession in the setting of accounting guidelines, it did so because the private sector was well equipped to do the job and the SEC saw no need to establish a duplicate staff of standard-setters. In doing so, as some observers have noted, it was deferring to a common-sense approach based largely on existing practice. But existing practice, as Carey notes, varied from corporation to corporation. Companies were expected to be consistent in their reporting from year to year, but companies were not expected to be completely consistent with one another. The notion of "comparability" by companies competing for capital, under which financial statements could be reasonably compared, simply did not exist in its present form.

As American business expanded after World War II, and the number of shareholders increased at a seemingly geometric rate, this lack of comparability began to be of considerable concern. Even earlier, however, the Institute's Committee on Accounting Procedure began to look toward establishing procedures that would enhance comparability, based on informal accounting research. Its pronouncements were not binding but were merely suggestions to the AICPA membership. Nonetheless, says Carey, the committee's "Accounting Research Bulletins soon had a visible influence on corporate accounting. While they did not establish uniform practices, they did gradually narrow the areas of difference by indicating preferred treatments among alternatives which up to then had had support in precedent." The SEC, in referring issues to the committee, lent its weight to the committee's undertakings.

Despite SEC support, the Committee on Accounting Procedure never did succeed in establishing a comprehensive body of generally accepted accounting principles. The Institute's then-president, Marquis G. Eaton, explained that generally accepted accounting principles weren't meant to be a uniform set of rules uniformly applicable in all circumstances. Instead, Eaton told a meeting of the Illinois Society of CPAs, "We know that 'generally accepted accounting principles' are broad concepts, evolving from the actual practices of business enterprises, and reflected in the literature of the accounting profession. . . . But we all know that in some areas there are equally acceptable alternative principles or procedures for the accounting treatment of identical items, one of which might result in an amount of net income reported in any one year widely different from the amount an alternative procedure might produce."

To some extent, as we've seen, alternative accounting procedures are still acceptable in some situations. "Highly intelligent people disagree strenuously on accounting issues," says Robert Van Riper, public relations director of the Financial Accounting Standards Board. "There's no parallel in other professions, which have accepted ways of doing things. In accounting, there's all kinds of room for opinion."

Yet the situation has improved. The accounting profession has made considerable progress in recent decades in codifying generally accepted accounting principles, today known familiarly as GAAP.

The Committee on Accounting Procedure, the target of

increasingly vocal criticism for permitting divergent alternative accounting practices, was succeeded in 1959 by the Accounting Principles Board (APB). Like the committee, the board was made up of volunteers, which limited its productivity. Like the committee, the board was supported by a research staff. Unlike the committee's pronouncements, however, the board's opinions were intended to have the weight of authority. That weight, however, was weakened by the fact that departures from the rules could be justified. Not only could they be justified, but in at least one notable instance, involving the investment tax credit, the SEC undermined the APB's authority by recognizing an alternative approach.

Both the Committee on Accounting Procedure and the Accounting Principles Board moved the profession toward widespread adoption of consistent accounting principles. But, in the opinion of many observers, the movement was too slow. By the late 1960's, more than three decades after the enactment of the securities laws that placed accounting rule-making in the private sector, "there was still," says John Carey, "no authoritative, comprehensive code of accounting principles in existence."

By the late 1960's, moreover, there was an increasing need for such a code. "The latter half of the decade of the sixties was a period of unprecedented stress for the individual members and institutions of the accounting profession," according to a Report of the Study on Establishment of Accounting Principles (the Wheat Committee) issued in March 1972. "Problems arising from the rapid expansion of accounting firms, the new issue boom, the development of increasingly complex and innovative business practices, and the corporate merger movement combined to create a wave of criticism of corporate financial reporting. This criticism came both from within and outside the profession, and much of it was focused upon the work of the APB."

Faced with increasing public criticism of (a) the opinion-shopping among corporations that resulted from the availability of different accounting standards, (b) failure to meet increasingly complex business needs, and (c) an apparent in-house control of accounting standards by the profession, the Wheat Committee had been asked by the AICPA to take a fresh look at why and how accounting standards should be established. After a year-long study, its 1972 report recommended the establishment of an independent standard-setting body. That body is the Financial Accounting Standards Board (FASB), whose seven members serve full-time, severing all connection with their prior occupations. "Today," says immediate past FASB chairman Donald J. Kirk, "FASB standards are binding on most companies and independent auditors, with stiff penalties for departures. The ethics rules of the American Institute of CPAs, the CPA licensing requirements of the fifty states, and the regulations of the Securities and Exchange Commission all mandate conformity with the Board's pronouncements."

FASB

With the backing of the AICPA, American Accounting Association, Financial Analysts Federation, Financial Executives Institute, and National Association of Accountants, a Financial Accounting Foundation was established in 1972. (Additional backing has since been secured from the Securities Industry Association.) The Foundation was empowered to organize both the Standards Board and an Advisory Council. The FASB itself got started in 1973, with a broad mission: to establish and improve standards of financial accounting and reporting for the guidance and education of the public, including issuers, auditors, and users of financial information.

Within this broad mandate, who takes precedence? Issuers or users? There has been considerable discussion over the years as to whether the primary purpose of financial accounting and reporting is to help management fulfill its accountability obligations or to provide information on which investment and credit decisions can be based. As reported in 1980 and 1985 Harris surveys of constituents' attitudes toward FASB, there is a definite shift toward acknowledging the needs of users. Only chief executive officers of private companies believe that management accountability is more important, in the 1985 survey; a decisive 59 to 31 percent of all respondents "believes that it is more critical to give a priority to generating information for investment and credit decisions."

Accounting standards, as the official FASB literature puts it, "are essential to the efficient functioning of the economy because decisions about the allocation of resources rely heavily on credible, concise, and understandable financial information. Financial information about the operations and financial position of individual entities also is used by the public in making various other kinds of decisions. To accomplish its mission, therefore, the FASB acts to:

1. Improve the usefulness of financial reporting by focusing on the primary characteristics of relevance and reliability and on the qualities of comparability and consistency;
2. Keep standards current to reflect changes in methods of doing business and changes in the economic environment;
3. Consider promptly any significant areas of deficiency in financial reporting that might be improved through the standard-setting process; and
4. Improve the common understanding of the nature and purposes of information contained in financial reports."

A noble purpose, and a tall order. How well has it been met?

Perhaps the best way to answer that question is to look

at what FASB has accomplished. Since its formation in 1973, the Board has issued numerous statements and interpretations, which establish financial accounting and reporting standards, and technical bulletins to provide guidance in implementing the standards.

Dissent is often stirred by FASB proposals. Toward the end of 1986, for example, the Board disclosed a proposed rule that would force companies to report consolidated results in their financial statements for all majority-owned subsidiaries. Right now, some companies follow this practice and others do not, making it difficult for lenders and investors to compare their financial conditions and prospects. Those who do not do so, and do not want to, have a reasonable argument. They complain that consolidating manufacturing with finance company operations, as an example, would result in a meaningless mix of apples and oranges, thereby confusing investors more than enlightening them.

Controversial or not, FASB rules do affect the bottom line and can, as a result, affect the way companies do business. In another recent example, the Board issued a proposed standard on accounting for income taxes that would change the way companies report the deferred effects of income taxes in their financial statements. Previously, once a company reported deferred tax, the amount was fixed on the company's books even if tax rates changed. Under the new standard, changes in tax rates and tax provisions are to be recognized in net income when the changes are enacted. With passage of the Tax Reform Act of 1986, and its sharp drop in corporate tax rates, this ruling could produce a big one-time boost in net worth for many companies.

Other major FASB statements deal with such areas as accounting and reporting of operating, capital, and leveraged leases; research and development costs; and the treatment of foreign currency transactions. Specific statements, many meant to reinforce the AICPA Industry Audit and

Accounting Guides, also deal with specific industry groups: franchising, cable TV, insurance, mortgage banking, real estate, etc. FASB "interpretations" clarify FASB statements, running the gamut from "accounting changes related to the cost of inventory" to "consolidation of a parent and its subsidiaries having different balance sheet dates." FASB technical bulletins either elaborate on previously issued standards or provide guidance in areas not directly covered by existing standards; technical bulletins tend to be fairly specific and range from "computer software costs" to "accounting for the effects of the Tax Reform Act of 1984 on deferred income taxes of stock life insurance enterprises."

Pensions

A closer look at pension accounting standards may put FASB's operations and its impact in clearer perspective.

At year-end 1985, FASB issued two pension-related statements: Statement 87, "Employers' Accounting for Pensions," establishes new reporting ground rules for corporate pension costs and obligations; Statement 88, "Employers' Accounting for Settlements and Curtailments of Defined Benefit Pension Plans and for Termination Benefits," deals with accounting for cutbacks of pension obligations in plan terminations, work force reductions, or early retirement programs. The titles are dry, but the contents are highly controversial.

In brief, Statement 87 requires companies to use a standardized method for measuring net periodic pension cost over each employee's service life, to disclose more information about the status of the plan in the notes to financial statements, and to recognize a liability when the accumulated benefit obligation exceeds the fair value of plan assets. Under Statement 88, previously deferred gains or losses are to be recognized in earnings when a pension obligation is settled. None of this may seem controversial.

But by requiring a standardized method to be used in computing pension expenses, as just one example, the standard precludes the use of different methods to meet different needs. What's more, some critics charge, the same rule puts accountants in the inappropriate role of actuaries, setting pension policy instead of reporting its results. The controversy was so sharp in the years preceding the pronouncements that *Institutional Investor* magazine called it "one of the most bitter wars in accounting history." With FASB's final adoption of the two standards, the cannons have ceased firing. But no one is quite sure just how the dust will settle.

Both standards became effective for employers' fiscal years beginning after December 15, 1986, except that both nonpublic companies with defined benefit plans covering 100 or fewer employees and companies with foreign-sponsored plans may delay implementation until 1989.

Some companies jumped on the bandwagon before they were required to do so. *The New York Times* reported "a surge of corporate enthusiasm" over the new measures in early 1986 among companies with overfunded pension plans, a condition common among major companies in the wake of the bull market. Companies with plan assets far exceeding plan obligations stood to gain many millions of dollars on the corporate bottom line. Underfunded plans, on the other hand, likely to incur higher pension costs under the new accounting standards, were delaying implementation of the new standards until the final deadline. "It's a drastic change for underfunded plans," says James J. Leisenring, FASB director of research and technical activities, "requiring the recording of a liability." According to a GAO study, 16 percent of pension plans are underfunded.

If stock market performance declines, however, today's cheerleaders may change their minds. A number of observers are taking a wait-and-see approach. "Year-to-year volatility. Major gains and losses. Dramatic increases and decreases in pension obligations. These are some of the phrases that come to mind when I consider understanding and applying the Financial Accounting Standard Board's (FASB's) Statements no. 87 and 88,'' says John Deming, KMG Main Hurdman's national director of accounting. "For many corporations pension cost could vary enough from year to year to significantly impact reported earnings.''

It's not only the corporate bottom line that will be affected. It may also be individual employees. If companies react by reducing funding for pension plans, employee benefits could be endangered. When the bottom line is at stake, shareholders' best interests may be pitted against pension recipients' best interests, with the shareholders winning out. In the real world, too, there's likely to be a problem with FASB-mandated differences between the accrual of pension expenses for financial statements and the actual funding of a plan. FASB was at pains to distinguish between the two, so as not to encroach on policymakers' turf. In fact, however, making two full pension calculations, one for funding purposes and one for financial reporting purposes, is impractical. Companies may therefore adopt for funding the method approved for financial reporting. This could slow fund buildup and could, in turn, ultimately reduce pension payments.

Whatever the ultimate impact of the pension standards, their adoption points to some major concerns surrounding FASB and its work.

Time Lag

Employers accounting for pension costs was placed on the agenda shortly after President Ford signed the Employee Retirement Income Security Act of 1974 (ERISA). Initial statements on accounting and reporting by defined benefit plans and on employer disclosure of pension information were released in 1980. Statements 87 and 88 were issued on December 1985. While not all pronouncements take quite that long—FASB says that major pronouncements typically take two years; others claim five to ten years is usual—the FASB has been criticized for the painstaking slowness of its decision-making.

That slowness, however, has its roots in a formal step-by-step process meant to take into account the views of FASB's far-flung constituency. The "due process" on major projects (naturally including an issue as complicated as pension accounting) goes through task force research, a discussion memorandum prepared as a basis for both written comment and oral presentations at a public hearing, the public hearing itself, staff analysis of oral and written comments, meetings of the Board, an exposure draft setting forth proposed standards, and further Board deliberation based on comments received on the exposure draft. Only after each of these steps is taken at least once—sometimes, extensive comment leads to a second round—is a Statement of Financial Accounting Standard issued.

The process takes so long, some critics have observed, that contrary accounting practices can be entrenched before a statement is issued. The Board has addressed this problem, at least in part, by establishing an Emerging Issues Task Force. The Task Force, chaired by FASB's research director, consists of practicing CPAs and industry representatives, with the chief accountant of the SEC sitting in; it meets every couple of months to identify and address new issues. Those issues may then be brought to the Board's attention, if broad-based standard-setting is considered essential. Or the Task Force can reach its own consensus on a preferable method of accounting for a new transaction; such consensus agreements are likely to be observed in practice (especially because the SEC recognizes Task Force consensus), eliminating the need for Board action and an FASB pronouncement.

The Task Force has achieved its aim of providing timely guidance on new issues. But it has also aroused some dissent. Jim Leisenring calls it "a form of de facto standard-setting body, identifying new issues, and debating and narrowing the range of acceptable practice.'' The problem here is that it's a de facto standard-setting body that doesn't adhere to due process, or widely publicize its decisions. In the end, suggests Keith Wishon of Price Waterhouse, writing in the *Journal of Accountancy*, ''the FASB will need to identify the common threads joining many of the issues and undertake projects to address the broader conceptual issues involved.''

This may be exactly what's taking place. The Task Force has spent a lot of time on new financial instruments. In an era when such instruments are proliferating, the Task Force setting can provide prompt attention and resolution of issues before widely disparate accounting practices are adopted by different entities. In mid-1986, however, new financial instruments became the focus of a new full-scale FASB project.

Who's in Charge Here?

The Emerging Issues Task Force, as we've seen, hears different voices. But what about FASB itself? It has been criticized as a voice of the Big Eight and AICPA. Remember the Metcalf Committee? A 1985 staff report to Congressman Dingell repeated the charges, saying, ''Generally accepted accounting principles are established by the FASB, an organization established, selected and funded by the AICPA and the Big Eight, with funding assistance from large corporate interests. The SEC has issued a rule requiring all publicly owned corporations to follow FASB standards. Does the SEC's delegation of its rulemaking authority to certain private interests serve the public? Can the FASB represent the public?''

In fact, as we've seen, the FASB has the backing of groups representing public accountants, management accountants, academics, financial analysts, etc. Its seven-man Board is drawn from industry and academia as well as the public practice of accounting. The qualifications for Board membership do not specify divergent backgrounds; they do specify that Board members have knowledge of accounting, finance, and business, plus a concern for the public interest in matters of financial accounting and reporting. In practice, although the bylaws do not require it, the Trustees attempt to maintain a mix, with three Board members from public accounting and the remainder divided among representatives of industry, academia, and a "user," such as a financial analyst or bank lending officer.

The makeup of the Board in 1987 is illustrative, although there is no user representative since Frank Block, a former vice-president of Bache Halsey Stuart Shields, retired at the end of 1985. At this writing the seven members include chairman Dennis R. Beresford, formerly of Ernst & Whinney; Victor H. Brown, formerly executive vice-president, chief financial officer, and director of the Firestone Tire & Rubber Company; Raymond C. Lauver, formerly of Price Waterhouse; David Mosso, formerly fiscal assistant secretary of the U.S. Treasury Department; C. Arthur Northrop, former controller and then treasurer of IBM Corp.; Robert J. Swieringa, former professor of accounting at the Johnson Graduate School of Management at Cornell University; and Arthur R. Wyatt, formerly of Arthur Andersen & Co. The wealth of experience brought from different backgrounds is important but, once on the Board, members are expected to vote their own minds rather than to express the views of any one group.

Representation, in any case, does not put an end to dissent. There is still a perception among members of the business community, according to a Financial Executives Institute position paper, "that their views have not been given adequate consideration in the standards-setting process." Or, as Roger B. Smith, chairman of the board of

General Motors and chairman of the accounting principles task force of the Business Roundtable, commented in voicing strong objections to the Board's pension proposals, "The FASB is out of touch with the business community."

The FEI paper calls for more business representation on both FASB and the Financial Accounting Foundation, FASB's parent body. As the primary users of financial statements and reports, the theory goes, business people can bring special insight to both the practical and the conceptual aspects of financial accounting and reporting. It may be in the interest of business to play a stronger role. But the Board, as we've noted, sees a broader responsibility; its mission is to all users of financial statements—investors, lenders, analysts, etc.—and not primarily to business.

The FASB, after weighing such criticism and surveying its constituents, does not believe its task is to heed conflicting factions so much as to bring neutrality and objectivity to the standard-setting process. "Independence is critical," says Rholan Larson, president of the Financial Accounting Foundation; "the process must be kept from undue influence by any constituent group." Or, as FASB's then-chairman, Donald J. Kirk, told the Dingell Committee in 1985, "The primary concern of the FASB is the relevance and reliability of the information that results, not the effect that the new rule may have on a particular interest. Accounting information must report economic activity as faithfully as possible, without coloring the image it communicates for the purpose of influencing behavior in some particular direction."

A Conceptual Framework

Neutrality as a concept is part of the framework of the FASB. So are relevance and reliability. Despite all the fine words, however, the FASB, like the Accounting Principles

Board before it, has had some difficulty coming to grips with the conceptual underpinnings of accounting.

One of the first tasks the FASB set itself was to establish a conceptual framework for its actions. The point: to reduce the need for what Michael O. Alexander, its former research director, described as "detailed, complex, asset-specific, industry-specific rules," the kind of rules that "are (1) so specific that they are not likely to be applicable to the next, unknown problem . . . , (2) so detailed that they almost invite compliance with the letter instead of the spirit, (3) so complex they are very difficult to understand and apply."

The task was more easily defined than accomplished. By June 1986, thirteen years after FASB's start, six statements of concepts had been formulated, starting with "objectives of financial reporting" and ending with "elements of financial statements." "One of the more significant accomplishments is the conceptual framework," Donald Kirk noted on the eve of his retirement as FASB chairman. "We put in place a framework—not necessarily a completely filled-in structure, but a framework." At the same time the Board, under Kirk's leadership, tended toward specificity. "History tells us," Kirk says, "that broad generalizations do not often result in reliable information. Today's environment seems to demand specificity."

There's some disappointment with the conceptual framework in its present form. "I think it's fair to say they struck out on the conceptual framework of financial reporting," says Dean Burton of the Columbia Business School. "The output-input relationship looks to me to be very dubious. The amount of resources that have gone into that project over a period of years and the outputs that have come from it seem to me to be disproportionate. I think that they have not dealt with many of the fundamental problems. They started out with a pretty good objective statement and then each additional statement in this conceptual framework project became less and less significant and I think ultimately they have given up the project." Dean Burton isn't alone in his assessment. Despite considerable feeling that more work is needed on this framework, however, work has stopped. One problem, says Donald Kirk, is the different views of different FASB constituencies. Although concepts are intended to be broad, there "is a business concern that a framework might be too specific, pointing the direction in solving specific problems. The business community prefers either very general standards or battling each issue separately."

Overload, or, Was This Standard Necessary?

Whether issued speedily or not, whether conceptually sound or not, Board pronouncements are subject to one repeated criticism: There are simply too many of them. The issue of "standards overload" has been raised time and time again since the FASB was founded in 1972. It may be less of a burning problem today than it once was, suggests Phil Chenok, president of AICPA, as FASB has communicated better with its constitutents. But "I'm concerned about how many standards can be issued and absorbed. People can accommodate comfortably to a certain amount of change. When there's too much, they have difficulty."

Overload, if it exists, may be in the eye of the beholder. Corporations don't particularly like rules, Don Kirk points out—the absence of rules permits opinion-shopping—but accounting firms struggling with issues appreciate guidance. Little wonder that, in its efforts to provide guidance, "the board is often caught between two disparate factions— one calling for more specific standards to eliminate any possibility of so-called creative accounting, and another criticizing a perceived overabundance of accounting standards."

In responding to the "overabundance" charge, Kirk points out that "we don't create, we respond to the demand. And we do screen requests, trying to minimize the number of official pronouncements." FASB receives many requests for action on various financial accounting and reporting topics from every segment of its constituency. It also responds to changes in the financial accounting reporting environment that may be brought about by new legislation and regulatory decisions. Items are placed on the agenda after considerable discussion, based on the pervasiveness of the problem, alternative solutions, technical feasibility, and practical consequences.

Despite the care taken to keep standards down, some observers think there are too many. Small accounting firms, in particular, if they're not dealing with the specific issues, may characterize FASB pronouncements as so much useless paper. "It's a small business issue, and a small CPA firm issue," says Jim Leisenring. "If you have a problem, you want guidance. If you don't, and see all the pronouncements, you question the flood of paper."

Differential Standards?

While Harris Polls taken of FASB constituents in 1980 and 1985 showed that most did not believe FASB was issuing too many pronouncements, the same polls also showed that respondents in smaller accounting firms felt that the FASB was not paying enough attention to the concerns of small businesses and small public accounting practitioners. "While the burden [of detailed standards] is shared by all companies," according to an AICPA Task Force on Accounting Standards Overload, "public companies have the potential benefit of performing more effectively in national capital markets when complying with these standards. Private companies and other small organizations receive no comparable benefit but still incur the cost of compliance with these standards."

Since small business may not need to provide as much information in financial statements as large corporations (user needs are different when there are no shareholders), and since it's small business and small CPA firms that seem to be overwhelmed by standards overload, proposals have been made for differential standards for small business and large.

Differential standards, however, may be a solution that aggravates the problem. For one thing, "small business" is a difficult term to define. A hundred-employee firm may be small in one industry, large in another. A new venture and a stable family-owned business may be the same size but have vastly different needs. For another, employing two sets of standards may undermine the credibility of the financial reporting system. "Two sets of standards would be a curious solution," says Jim Leisenring, "one that wouldn't make applying standards any easier."

But differential standards can be broken down in two ways. The first, differential disclosure, an optional exemption from certain disclosures for privately owned companies, is already accepted by FASB in certain specific areas. "Earnings per share was information required of all corporations," notes Sam Derieux, chairman of the AICPA Task Force on Accounting Standards Overload, "yet it has absolutely no meaning in a closely held business where an individual owns half or all of the business. It's not that it's difficult to do, but it's meaningless clutter. The FASB has suspended this rule for nonpublic companies."

Differential measurement, applying simplified or at least different measurement or recognition rules to specific transactions based on the criteria of relevance to users and cost-benefit considerations, is another issue. While many people—including a sizable majority of the AICPA Council members surveyed in spring 1986—believe that differential measurement alternatives are appropriate for certain entities, the Board believes that differential measurement, based solely on the size of entities, "would have an adverse effect both on companies required to recognize certain transactions and on those exempted. Exempting certain companies from recognition would inevitably lead to questions concerning the integrity of their financial statements." Moreover, in Don Kirk's words, "At some point differential measurement becomes indistinguishable from two sets of generally accepted accounting principles." The Board has not officially ruled out the possibility of differential measurement but, in the opinion of Dennis Beresford, current FASB chairman, "Most people believe differential measurement rules—different accounting procedures for different size companies—are not a good idea." The public interest is best served in this view, which may be out of step with majority opinion, by standards that result in accounting for similar transactions similarly, regardless of company size.

Simplification of standards—for companies of every size—could help. But as long as small businesses enter into transactions that are as complicated as those of big business (complicated leasing arrangements are just one example), small business will face complex accounting problems.

Meanwhile, the FASB is trying to close the gap with its small business constituents by improving communication. A Small Business Advisory Group (SBAG) was established in 1984 to provide a "front line" of contact with the small business community. SBAG is involved before projects are added to the Board's agenda, during the development of staff recommendations, and during preparation of exposure drafts. On all projects, says a special report to the Board of Trustees of the Financial Accounting Foundations, the Board will "seek answers to the following with regard to whether small businesses should be treated differently from large corporations:

- Whether the different treatment would alleviate 'standards overload'—or contribute to it by providing two solutions instead of one;

- Whether a proposed solution would enhance or diminish the credibility of financial reporting;
- Whether there is persuasive evidence that user needs are different for different entities or that the costs outweigh the benefits;
- Whether there is a difference in the economic basis of a transaction for different entities."

Members of the Small Business Advisory Group also receive all information that is sent to the Emerging Issues Task Force (EITF), and care is taken to ensure that actions by the EITF do not pose unexpected implications for small business.

In the Board's view, in short, the best way to alleviate small business concerns about standards overload is to ensure that the views of small business are heard and heeded. It remains to be seen whether expanded dialogue adequately addresses the issue.

The Governmental Accounting Standards Board

In 1897, Ernest Reckitt wrote in his "Reminiscences of Early Days of the Accounting Profession in Illinois," in what he believed to be probably the first municipal audit, he was invited to make a "spot audit" of the books of the City of Chicago. Reckitt found a "disordered mass" of bonds and interest coupons, so disordered that "to have attempted to put them in numerical order, so as to commence any audit, would have been a greater task than Hercules undertook in cleaning out the 'Augean Stables.' " The city determined "to let 'Bygones be Bygones' and to inaugurate better methods which would prevent in the future those irregularities which, it was feared, had existed in the past."

*   *   *

In some respects private-sector accounting and public-sector accounting are very similar. Irregularities were not uncommon in either arena in the late nineteenth century because neither accounting nor auditing standards existed in written form in the profession's early years. Today they do. But there are also differences in accounting practices and financial reporting standards between the private sector and the public sector. And there is some controversy over who has jurisdiction for what.

Accounting standards were well established in the private sector first, starting with the AICPA's Committee on Accounting Procedures, working through the Accounting Principles Board, and continuing with the establishment of the Financial Accounting Standards Board in 1972. Accounting standards for state and local government units, meanwhile, were developed by the National Council of Governmental Accounting (NCGA) sponsored by the Municipal Finance Officer's Association; AICPA incorporated the NCGA standards within its governmental accounting guide. But, says Martin Ives, vice-chairman and director of research of the Governmental Accounting Standards Board, NCGA was a voluntary part-time body and "there were a lot of holes in the literature." Moreover, notes Wallace E. Olson, former AICPA president, in the *Accounting Profession: Years of Trial*, "Studies by several of the National CPA firms revealed that [the standards] were not being consistently followed."

The inadequacy of governmental standard-setting led to growing dissatisfaction and a 1979 congressional proposal for a federally financed governmental accounting standards board. The profession was opposed to government intervention in standard-setting and suggested, instead, that FASB was the logical body to set standards for both private enterprise and governmental bodies. As a 1980 report by the Financial Accounting Foundation puts it, "A single standard-setting body is most likely to produce accounting standards that are consistent with one another and in relation to a framework of objectives, concepts, and other agreed-on fundamentals." State and local governmental representatives, however, objected to both federal and FASB domination. There was some belief, as the FAF noted, that FASB "has a business bias, lacks government expertise, and lacks credibility among government financial officials, and that its involvement would amount to the private sector regulating government." The end result, after several years of negotiation: formation of the Governmental Accounting Standards Board in 1984 as an independent entity, parallel to FASB under the Financial Accounting Foundation umbrella.

The GASB is a five-member body, backed by a research staff, whose chairman and vice-chairman serve full-time; the other members serve on a part-time basis and may hold other jobs as well. All are required to have knowledge of governmental accounting and finance and a concern for the public interest in matters of financial accounting and reporting. The makeup of the initial Board is interesting: James F. Antonio, chairman, is former state auditor of Missouri. Martin Ives, vice-chairman, is former first deputy comptroller for the City of New York and the man largely credited with rescuing New York from its fiscal crisis. Philip L. Defliese, former chairman and managing partner of Coopers & Lybrand, is currently professor of accounting at Columbia University. W. Gary Harmer is administrator of educational resources for the Salt Lake City School District. And Elmer B. Staats is a former comptroller general of the United States.

GASB's accounting standards apply only to state and local governments; the federal government, as we shall see, has rules of its own. Comptroller General Charles Bowsher has suggested that accounting standards should be uniform at every level of government. Such uniformity would enhance the political process, as elected officials could carry budget and accounting know-how from one level of government to the next, as well as accountability. But federal/ state/local uniformity is not on anyone's agenda and does not appear likely to happen soon.

GASB's procedures, like FASB's, are carefully designed to ensure due process and to encourage broad public participation in the standards-setting process. Major projects proceed deliberately through preliminary research to define the issue, task force study, the issuance of a discussion memorandum including alternative solutions, a public hearing, an exposure draft of a proposed statement for public comment prior to final adoption, and then, at last, issuance of a final Statement. GASB also, like FASB, may issue Technical Bulletins designed to provide timely guidance on issues of a limited scope. And it may issue Statements of Governmental Accounting Concepts and Interpretations.

Like FASB, too, the GASB is concerned with the impact of its standards on smaller entities. To make sure that small governments have a voice in due process, GASB has established a Small Governments Task Force including both finance officials from small municipalities and CPAs who conduct audits of small municipalities. In addition to listening to the voice of small government, the task force tries to make compliance a little less onerous and keep costs down. As an example, small pension plans are required to make calculations somewhat less frequently than larger plans.

Such measures may help gain acceptance for the Board's pronouncements. The authority to require that GAAP be followed rests with the individual states; GASB can't compel adherence. Many state and local governments have had a pretty poor record over the years for fiscal responsibility. It's gratifying to note, therefore, that recent surveys show greater adherence than had been believed. In a survey of cities, counties, and school districts, conducted for GASB in 1986 by Robert W. Ingram and Walter A. Rob-

bins of the School of Accountancy, University of Ala-
bama, 93.8 percent of the cities, 82.9 percent of the counties,
and 88.8 percent of the school districts reported that their
financial statements were audited in accordance with GAAP;
about a third had had their first GAAP audit within the
preceding five years. And, in a survey of states conducted at the University of Kentucky for the Council of
State Governments, twenty-six out of the fifty reported
GAAP statements; other sources indicate that another fifteen or so are moving in this direction. GAAP standards
aren't mandated but, in the wake of the New York City
fiscal crisis, bond-rating agencies have been pushing for
properly prepared and audited financial statements.

The GASB had its first meeting in mid-1984, but it
wasn't until May 1986 that the AICPA officially designated the GASB as the "body to establish financial accounting principles for state and local governmental entities"
under its Code of Ethics. Nonetheless, GASB has made
some important strides.

A major project on GASB's initial agenda was completed in mid-1985 with the publication of the first codification of standards pertaining specifically to governmental
entities. This codification included many NCGA standards,
since they remain in effect until they are amended or
superceded by the GASB.

The next major project, and the highest priority on
GASB's agenda right now, is an examination of the fundamental underpinnings of financial reporting by governments:
When is a revenue a revenue, an expenditure an expenditure? What happens to your tax dollars? Tentative conclusions, reached after field tests to determine the effect on
governments of varying sizes, adopt a "flow of total financial resources" measurement focus which measures the
accumulation of financial resources and the incurrence of
liabilities against those resources, regardless of when cash
is received or disbursed.

Tax revenues would be recognized when some action is taken by the government to demand or exact the taxes—in other words, regardless of when the money is actually received. Expenditures, similarly, would be recognized when the liability is incurred regardless of when cash is actually paid out. This "total financial resources approach, with a heavier degree of accrual accounting," says Martin Ives, "is a major conceptual change from NCGA's measure of current financial resources. Under the current standard, if a legislature doesn't appropriate funds for pensions, they are not reported. Under the tentative new standard, earned pensions would have to be reported as expenditures even if they were not funded in a particular period." Similarly, GASB has tentatively concluded that claims and judgments against a government should be recognized when the events occur rather than when payments are actually made. Claims may not be settled for five years, Ives points out, but a reasonable estimate of costs can be based on past experience. Due process on the measurement item had reached the stage of an exposure document draft by the beginning of 1987.

Another major priority for GASB is a reexamination of the financial reporting structure. Among the questions here: How do you define an entity? Is the New Jersey Turnpike or the Meadowland Sports Authority, for example, part of the State of New Jersey? Or is each a separate entity for financial reporting purposes? Once you define the entity, what does that entity need to report and how should it be reported?

And the third major priority, and possibly the most controversial, is accounting for pensions.

FASB vs. GASB?

According to the hierarchy of generally accepted accounting principles, GASB rules apply first to governmental bodies. If GASB has not specified the accounting treatment of a transaction or event, then FASB rules apply. When FASB issued its Statement 87, on pensions, GASB had not yet acted and the FASB ruling should have applied to governmental entities. But GASB had started its work on pension disclosure and expected its standard to be different. GASB, therefore, in an action that didn't sit well with everyone, issued a statement telling government entities not to follow FASB 87. Today, GASB is going ahead with its independent work on standards for pension disclosures and pension accounting.

Some people feel that a single set of standards should apply in the private and the public sectors. Columbia's Dean Burton, for example, "was really opposed to a separate government accounting standards board; the differences that arise out of different constituencies and different objectives could have been handled, should have been handled through a single board." Others feel that private enterprises and government entities have different purposes and should, therefore, adhere to different standards. "We take the position that government is in business forever," Ives notes. "Because we start with a different perspective, we come up with a different answer."

In the pension area this means that "FASB's calculations in Statement 87 are based on the settlement rate, a rate that changes every year. We agree with the actuarial approach, using a long-range perspective," Ives continues, "because we think pension plans should be long-range and shouldn't fluctuate with interest rates. Our approach results in a much larger obligation." One reason the obligation is so much larger is that GASB's approach considers the effect of salary increases through all the years leading to retirement. In government, as the Board notes, "pension plans are rarely terminated and employees are widely regarded as having a right to benefits earned."

The GASB applies its governmental perspective not only to transactions, such as pensions, but to entities as well. It is beginning to look at public colleges and universities, for example, to see if special accounting standards are needed. As a first step, it is sponsoring academic research to see if different users have different needs. Even if they don't, there may be differences in accountability. Most public colleges, for example, following existing governmental standards, do not report depreciation expense. Private colleges, following GAAP, do. While it may be logical for the private sector and the public sector to follow different accounting rules—there is a difference between General Motors and the City of New York—not everyone sees the logic when it comes to identical institutions which happen to be in the different sectors. In a highly critical article, *Forbes* magazine points out that different accounting standards for identical entities, whether those entities are colleges or hospitals or utilities, can lead to nothing but confusion.

It's a complex situation. Different standards on the same subject can be justified by different users—"standards are not God-given truths," says Rholan Larson, president of the Financial Accounting Foundation—yet many feel that standards should be harmonized. If they're *not* harmonized, then, at the very least, duplication and overlap should be reduced to a bare minimum. To this end, says Larson, the trustees are becoming much more involved with monitoring the process.

Back in 1981, when a Governmental Accounting Standards Board was first being considered, the trustees recognized that "a two-board structure would entail various jurisdictional and overlap issues and that the Foundation would have ultimate responsibility to determine a mechanism to bring about final resolution of conflicts that the GASB and FASB cannot work out between themselves." That conflict, coming to a head over the pension issue and exacerbated by GASB's anticipated pronouncements on colleges, led the trustees to appoint a Structure Committee, which has issued two sets of recommendations. The first suggests an organizational framework with an executive vice-president, reporting directly to the trustees, handling administration for both Boards. This recommendation has been implemented.

The second, a Report to Trustees Regarding Consistent Standards by FASB and GASB, issued in December 1986, concluded, "The problem is not one of deciding whether a particular entity is or is not a governmental entity. . . . The problem (or, more precisely, at this point in time, the *potential* problem) is that the two Boards, acting entirely within their defined jurisdiction, can establish different standards for the same types of transactions (e.g., pension costs and depreciation) and entities (e.g., utilities and hospitals) not justified by the fact that there are differences in circumstances." Moreover, "The perception of, and respect for, the entire standards setting process is likely to be adversely affected if the two Boards establish different standards for what are, or what are perceived to be, the same activities, transactions or circumstances."

For these reasons, the Committee recommends: (1) increased communication between the two Boards; (2) avoidance of duplication in research; (3) an explanation to the trustees when one Board adds an item to its agenda that had already been tackled by the other Board; and (4) justification for any standard that differs from a standard on the same issue already promulgated by the other Board. The Committee also specifically recommended that a communication plan be developed to implement items (1) and (2); the chairman of the two Boards met in early 1987 to work out appropriate procedures.

Will the Structure Committee recommendations help to resolve differences between the two Boards? Maybe. Since each Board sees its mission somewhat differently, some differences may remain.

Donald Kirk, past chairman of FASB, defines its mission as "decision-usefulness." Martin Ives, vice-chairman of GASB, talks in terms of accountability. Financial reports in the private sector, in other words, should meet the needs of investors and creditors, or those who base economic decisions on the information. Financial reports in the public sector, where, as Ives puts it, "the bottom line ought to be zero," should demonstrate compliance with the entity's budget and accountability to the taxpayer. The major difference is that private enterprise is out to make a profit, to maximize return to owners; government's goal is "to provide optimal service within available resources." The difference in goals, GASB believes, leads to inevitable differences in financial reporting and in reporting standards. Despite the structure committee's recommendations, says Ives, all of GASB's members believe that if projects are important to government, they will be put on the agenda even if FASB has previously issued a pronouncement.

The battles over turf, it seems, are not yet at an end. The initial jurisdiction agreement provided that GASB would establish standards for governmental entities while FASB establishes standards for other than governmental entities. But what is a governmental entity? Is it only a general-purpose state or local government? Or does it include special-purpose organizations, such as schools and hospitals, operated by government? Martin Ives claims that the intent was always to include such special-purpose entities in GASB's jurisdiction. The end result, however, may be different accounting standards for similar entities. Does it matter? Does anyone need to compare the financial statements of a public hospital and a private hospital? The GASB is still studying the issue of comparability. But opinion among observers is divided. Different answers seem appropriate in different situations. Legislatures and bond issuers, for example, would compare governments with governments and not with the private sector. But what about bond buyers? They might well make a comparison in deciding whether to buy a corporate or a municipal issue. The arguments go back and forth.

The original agreement establishing GASB called for a mandatory review of its operations after five years. After the review, which should take place in 1989, the Financial Accounting Foundation anticipates facing several choices: to combine FASB and GASB into a single board, to create a separate oversight Foundation for GASB, to continue the two Boards under a modified structure, or to leave the two-board structure as it currently stands. Perhaps some answers will become clearer after this review. The jurisdictional issue, meanwhile, is unresolved.

6

The Auditor's Role: Expectation and Reality

Audits may be required by law, but "the statutory audit requirement is of little significance in our economy. Clients should see benefits exceeding the cost," says Robert K. Elliot of Peat Marwick. "Take a major company with capitalization in excess of $20 billion. If an audit improves the cost of capital by twenty basis points, that would be $40 million a year—an amount that far exceeds the auditor's fee."

"He who audits, gets no plaudits" is an old ditty that may ring all too true to many auditors in the late 1980's. While performing an audit is the primary accounting function, the one function generally reserved to certified public accountants—audits of publicly held companies by independent auditors are required under the federal Securities Acts of 1933 and 1934—there is considerable confusion today as to just what an audit is supposed to accomplish and just what an auditor is expected to do. The public seems to have one understanding, the profession another.

The dictionary definition is straightforward. According to Barron's *Dictionary of Finance and Investment Terms*, an audit is "professional examination and verification of a company's accounting documents and supporting data for the purpose of rendering an opinion as to their fairness, consistency, and conformity with generally accepted accounting principles."

To the profession, the definition is perfectly clear. In the words of Philip B. Chenok, president of AICPA, "The primary purpose of an audit is to provide reasonable assurance that the financial statements are fairly presented in conformity with generally accepted accounting principles and that they are consistently applied. Auditors' opinions do not deal with the competence or quality of a company's management, the ongoing profitability of a company, or indeed the wisdom of investing in a particular company." Or, as Clarence Sampson, chief accountant of the SEC, puts it, "If a company is having trouble because of an industry downturn, the auditor has no present responsibility to say so, as long as the financial statements are fair. Similarly, if a company is taking unreasonable risks, the auditor has no present responsibility to say so unless those risks would jeopardize recoverability of assets."

Yet many members of the public believe that this is exactly what the auditor's responsibility is; they interpret an unqualified opinion as conferring a "clean bill of health," a "Good Housekeeping seal of approval" indicating that the company is sound. If they then invest in that company and suffer a loss, they may blame the auditor. This latter view is echoed in the words of Representative John D. Dingell, chairman of the Energy and Commerce Committee and of its Subcommittee on Oversight and Investigations: "Along with the choice to become an accountant comes a responsibility and commitment to prevent fraud and to provide the public with an independent and fair assessment of a corporation's financial status." The auditor, in Chief Justice Warren Burger's words, is a "public watchdog." As such, according to Burger, he or she should blow the whistle on corporate wrongdoing and provide an early warning system for the public on management competence and company stability.

The question of the auditor as whistle-blower, as we shall see, is arguable. But everyone seems to agree that the audit function is essential and that the auditor, in performing that function, must be both objective and independent in serving the public interest. Again, there's a question of definition. Assuming that the auditor must be independent in both fact and appearance, does performing management advisory services for an audit client compromise the appearance of independence? As noted in Chapter 2, many people say that it does. But saying so, according to Duane Kullberg, chairman of Arthur Andersen, "walks right by the basic question of conflict in an auditor getting paid by the company whose financial statement he's asked to judge. I can overcome that challenge, and remain independent. And I can do management consulting and remain independent." (Over the years, it should be noted, a couple of critics have suggested that auditors should *not* be paid by the audit client but that they should be an arm of government, paid by government. The assumption seems to be that "government" is an objective entity, with no self-interest. This proposal has never come close to adoption.) In any case, because they are knowledgeable about their client's business, CPAs are well equipped to provide a variety of advisory services for their clients; forbidding them to do so would deprive American business of their skill and expertise.

Everyone also seems to agree that the audit function is essential, because it ensures the integrity of the financial information on which our economic system depends. But how much assurance is expected? Whose expectation is correct? Are auditors responsible for ferreting out every instance of fraud? For assessing the stability of a company? Or are they responsible solely for examining the financial statements provided by management and determining if those statements are fairly presented?

The answer—or at least the level of public expectation as to auditor performance—may vary with the times. Problem audits tend to be associated with problem industries. In the 1970's it was real estate; then it was defense contractors; more recently it has been banks and thrifts.

"These industries generally were in transition, because of deregulation, disinflation or other reasons," Comptroller General Charles Bowsher told the Dingell Committee, "and sometimes the auditors did not become aware of the risks, changes and problems being experienced by the companies within these industries until it was too late. . . . As a result the public often has had no early warning regarding the precarious condition of some of these firms."

Sometimes political factors play a role along with economic factors. Bob Elliot of Peat Marwick notes that Congress gets involved two years after the bottom of every economic cycle. After an economic trough, when many companies fail, the accountants are blamed. It happened with the Moss-Metcalf hearings of the mid-1970's; it's happening with the Brooks-Dingell hearings of the mid-1980's; it will happen again.

But whether problem audits are cyclical or not, the profession is deeply concerned about the current crisis in credibility. Most CPAs believe that it may be virtually impossible to detect fraud if management is in collusion. This was evident as far back as 1938, when officers of McKesson & Robbins concealed a multimillion-dollar theft by providing auditors with forged inventory sheets, purchase invoices, customer accounts, and shipping documents. But what if the auditors do discover fraud? And what steps should be taken if gross incompetence is detected?

More can and should be done, both to educate the public as to the auditor's responsibility and to redefine that responsibility. As a result of recent revelations of management fraud that was not caught by the independent auditors, says the Institute's 1985–86 chairman Herman J. Lowe of H. J. Lowe & Company in Baton Rouge, Louisiana, "at least three major questions and challenges must be dealt with by the profession:

• The auditor's responsibility for the prevention and detection of fraud;

- The auditor's responsibility to provide an 'early warning' about significant risks and uncertainties that may affect a business entity's future prospects;
- The ability of the profession to improve auditor performance without direct intervention by the federal government.''

In view of what has been aptly called a major expectation gap, the audit function deserves careful examination. This chapter will focus on business failure and the auditor's responsibility, on the current litigation crisis, on the possibility of government intervention, and on self-regulation by a concerned profession.

Business Failure/Audit Failure

> I am not allowed to run the train
> the whistle I can not blow.
> I am not allowed to say
> how far the cars can go.
> I am not allowed to shoot off steam
> nor even clang the bell.
> But let it jump the railroad track,
> then see who catches Hell.
> —*Anonymous*

Companies have always failed, of course, and will always fail. Some fail as a result of management fraud, some from management incompetence, some because of economic factors beyond their control. Whatever the reason, failure can occur shortly after an auditor issues an unqualified opinion on the financial statements. Is a business failure, then, necessarily an audit failure? The accounting profession says no. There may be no way the auditors can uncover fraud if management is in collusion. There may be no way to ascertain economic conditions that will undermine a company's stability in the future. Financial statements are, of necessity, historical documents and not forecasts. But, in our current litigious atmosphere, people are suing over such issues. Not all the suits are justified, and many settlements are reached simply to avoid the cost and disruption of resisting suits. Whether or not the suits were justified, whether or not the firms were guilty as charged, according to the SEC, between 1980 and early 1985 the Big Eight accounting firms paid out over $175 million in settlements and judgments in cases over disputed audits.

Business failures, of course, do not always lead to lawsuits, nor do they always stem from fraud. But a Dingell subcommittee staff report of 1985 points to a number of fraud-related business failures that could be construed as audit failures. In 1982, for example, Arthur Andersen issued a clean opinion on the financial statements of Drysdale Government Securities, a company that the SEC contends was actually insolvent the day it opened. One lawsuit that followed the Drydale collapse was settled out of court; another went to trial and its verdict, against the accounting firm, was upheld by the Supreme Court. In January 1984, Ernst & Whinney issued an unqualified opinion on the 1982 financial statements of Continental Illinois; by May the bank was undergoing a run on deposits and by July the FDIC was arranging a rescue operation. Both the FDIC and a group of shareholders sued Ernst & Whinney; the case came to trial in spring 1987.

The subcommittee staff lists a series of business frauds going back for a decade—Frigitemp, Penn Square Bank, E.S.M., Baldwin United—and claims knowledge of at least forty more. In some of these cases, the auditors were sued by investors and creditors seeking both to recover their money and to attach blame. Sometimes, as in the E.S.M. case, the auditors are clearly culpable; the Alexander Grant partner supervising the audit admitted taking "loans" from the client and concealing E.S.M.'s poor financial condition. Sometimes the auditors are clearly innocent, victims of the "deep pockets" syndrome in which lawsuits are launched against anyone, however remotely connected, with the capacity to pay. Sometimes the situation is arguable.

Despite the wide publicity given to these failures and others like them, in any case, the cold hard statistics can comfort the accounting profession. According to a report issued in the summer of 1986 by a committee of the AICPA, CPA firms that are members of the SEC Practice Section were accused of alleged audit failures in connection with the audits of 160 public companies in the preceding six years. Another 43 cases came up the next year. In total, this number (now 203) represents a small fraction of 1 percent of the more than sixty thousand audits performed during the period.

Businesses fail for a variety of reasons that are unrelated to the financial reporting process—because of poor management, societal or technological developments, domestic and foreign competition, and changes in the economy. The independent audit, by bringing professional oversight to the financial reporting process, can serve to deter the issuance of misleading financial statements by management. But as the AICPA has noted, "The role of the independent auditor is not to guarantee that investors and creditors will not make bad judgments and suffer losses. Neither is it to advise users of financial statements on the desirability of investing in or lending to a company." Those roles are more properly filled by investment advisers and rating agencies; it's interesting to note, in passing, that neither of these seems to be as subject to lawsuits in business failures as are CPAs.

But what if the auditor detects early warning signals of impending failure? What, then, is the auditor's responsibility? Some, including some of the congressional investigators, maintain that it is then the auditor's responsibility to warn the investing public. Others point out that hard evidence had better be in hand before such a warning is issued. They also caution that such a warning in itself could prove to be a self-fulfilling prophecy. If the evidence could be construed as insufficient, or if the warning itself provoked rapid selling of shares and a consequent decline in price, the auditors could be liable to civil suit. Just the threat of public whistle-blowing, moreover, would put the auditor in an adversarial position with management, a position that would make securing information from management very difficult.

The issue, like the modern audit itself, is complex. The growing use of the computer, which presents problems in documentation while it speeds the audit process, also opens up avenues for fraud. At the very least, computers make control more difficult to achieve and maintain. Audit complexity has also grown, as former Comptroller General Elmer B. Staats told the Institute of Internal Auditors in June 1986, with organizational complexity—mergers, internationalization, technological change, innovative financing arrangements, changing legislative and regulatory environments.

Contemporary audit practices have the auditors testing data within a framework of internal controls. If the auditor were to be responsible for providing early warning signals of business failure, or for detecting any and all evidence of fraud down to purloined paper clips, then audits would of necessity become increasingly lengthy, as every piece of paper was examined, and increasingly costly.

Right now, in any case (and probably to the surprise of some auditors), auditors *are* responsible for detecting errors and irregularities that would be material to the financial statements being examined. "Material" is technically defined as anything important enough to change or influence the judgment of a reasonable person who is relying on the financial statements. In fact, it is frequently viewed as anything that could significantly affect the bottom line. Either way, it is a relative standard, because the error (or, for that matter, the fraud) that could put the corner grocery store out of business might have no impact at all on the overall health of a Fortune 500 corporation. This is clearly an area where the auditor's judgment must come into play. What's important, however, is that the auditor is expected to detect irregularities and to make a judgment about their significance. What's important, too, is that the Auditing Standards Board of the AICPA is redefining the rules so that this responsibility can't be ignored or misinterpreted. There will be a clear requirement, says Dan Guy, AICPA's vice-president of auditing, "to do a lot of work in response to so-called red flags or worrying signs." The quality of professional skepticism, a necessary ingredient in any audit, will be reinforced.

Unfortunately, professional skepticism is sometimes lacking. Sometimes it's a matter of a junior auditor unquestioningly accepting management representations that should be questioned. Sometimes it's a senior audit team cutting corners in the interest of cutting costs. Whatever the cause, serious concerns have surfaced about substandard audits. A 1986 report by the House of Representatives Committee on Government Operations (the Brooks Committee) states, "The committee's recent review documents that an estimated *34 percent* of CPA audits of Federal financial assistance funds fail to meet generally accepted government auditing standards." Audits of government agencies, funds, and programs must meet special rules. Audits of government funds are also subject to a bidding process, which may create temptations to cut corners. But audits of public agencies may more easily be examined than audits of companies, even publicly held companies, in the private sector. Some observers suspect that the pattern of substandard work in the public sector may have a mirror image in the private sector. If this is so, the increased self-regulatory efforts that are currently under way will be more important than ever.

Liability and Litigation

As noted, investors and creditors are not sitting still when businesses go under; increasingly, they are turning to the auditors to make their losses good. The increase in civil suits against accounting firms is part of the general increase in civil liability suits in an increasingly litigious era.

Most worrisome to the profession is the recent broad extension of liability, in some jurisdictions, to seemingly limitless numbers of third parties. Accountants and other professionals have always been liable for damage to parties with which they have direct contractual relationships. Under federal securities laws, moreover, accountants may be liable for recklessness to third parties under some circumstances. But some current court decisions are going beyond these definitions of liability.

The situation varies from state to state. In California, an appeals court recently allowed a real estate developer to bring suit against an accounting firm on the grounds that the developer had relied on the firm's audit of a mortgage company; when the mortgage company failed to meet its obligations, the developer looked to the CPAs to make good. CPAs find such conclusions disheartening; how can they know, they ask, what use such unrelated third parties will want to make of a client's financial statements? More encouraging, from the point of view of the profession, is the 1985 New York Court of Appeals ruling in the Credit Alliance case. In that instance, the court ruled that the extent of a CPA firm's liability to nonclients in the preparation of financial reports depends on whether the firm knew the reports would be used and relied upon for a particular purpose.

Concerned about the rapidly growing number of lawsuits in general, and the extension of liability in particular, the AICPA Special Committee on Accountants' Legal Liability, headed by Ray J. Groves, chairman of Ernst & Whinney and a former chairman of AICPA, has instituted a program for legislative reform. The program has five key points:

1. Replacing the rule of "joint and several" liability, under which a claimant can collect 100 percent of the damages from a defendant who may be only 5 percent responsible (the so-called "deep pockets" syndrome), with "several" liability, under which damages would be limited to a proportionate share of the loss. Several states, including California, have already taken legislative action in this direction.

2. Supporting the "privity" concept, which denies the right to sue to non–contractually related third parties with whom the accountant has no direct relationship. Here the Institute endorses the privity rule established by the New York Court of Appeals and opposes the "foreseeability" rule adopted in New Jersey and a few other states, which allows a negligence suit to be brought by any third party whose reliance on financial statements could reasonably have been foreseen by the accountant. (It's not necessarily an either-or proposition. SEC Commissioner Joseph Grundfest, in an interview with *Accounting Practices & Regulations*, suggested an alternative, an in-between measure that would identify an audit as two distinct services: the performance of the audit itself plus a warranty that the audit can be relied upon. It's an interesting suggestion.)

3. Supporting corrective legislation to amend federal and state RICO (the Racketeer Influenced and Corrupt Organizations Act) statutes. RICO was designed to protect legitimate business from infiltration or dishonest acts by organized crime. But it has been used (some would say misused) by many others, tempted by its automatic treble damages and award of legal fees, in ordinary commercial litigation. The Institute's proposal, which came very close to adoption by the Congress in late 1986, would restrict RICO cases to businesses and individuals who have been

convicted of criminal violations under the act. This legislation would accomplish two aims: treble damages would be restricted to those who are actually involved in criminal activities, and the term "racketeer" would not be unfairly applied to others.

4. Deterring the increasing numbers of frivolous suits and attorneys' fee arrangements that provide incentive to file lawsuits against "deep pocket" defendants regardless of merit. Such deterrence could take several forms, including adoption of British procedures, which impose the costs of litigation on the losing party; imposing sanctions on those who bring baseless suits; limiting contingency fees, which may encourage attorneys to bring suit; abolishing punitive damages; and reducing the statute of limitations for negligence actions.

5. Clarifying the standard under which auditors may be held secondarily liable for aiding and abetting a violation of law by those who are primarily responsible. Specifically, the AICPA supports legislative reforms to require a finding of actual knowledge by the CPA of the primary party's wrongdoing, as opposed to reckless disregard of facts which would have led to the auditor's discovery of such wrongdoing. Some courts do require actual auditor knowledge of the wrongdoing, but uncertainty in this area breeds uncertain results, stimulates more litigation, and increases the rate of settlement to avoid the risk of an uncertain outcome.

Many firms will settle litigants' claims rather than go to court. But it's a no-win situation, says Howard Lutz, a partner in Schneider & Shuster in Denver and president of the Colorado Society of CPAs. "We are sued regularly, but we can't sue a client for a fee or he will countersue on some basis, impairing our ability to get insurance. Simply being named in a lawsuit affects our insurance as well as our reputation. Lawyers know this, and clients are learning. We have no stick to swing."

Liability Insurance

While changing liability laws state by state is of paramount importance, resolving the insurance crunch is also important. Accounting firms of all sizes, along with other professionals and many businesses, are being squeezed by higher premiums and restricted (or unavailable) insurance coverage. Several steps have been taken. The AICPA's nationwide professional liability insurance program covers more than fifteen thousand firms. A number of the nation's largest firms, excluding the Big Eight with their big liability exposure through their audits of large numbers of publicly held companies, have formed their own captive insurance company based in Hamilton, Bermuda. Most of the Big Eight themselves have formed a Barbados-based captive company. A risk retention group licensed in Delaware under new federal law plans to offer insurance nationwide, concentrating on firms with fewer than fifty CPAs. The California Society of CPAs has launched its own self-insurance company, California Accountants Mutual Insurance Company. The AICPA is looking into whether a national captive insurance company should be formed.

Meanwhile, loss prevention measures are increasingly important. Such measures involve carefully drafting engagement letters to spell out both any potential problem areas and the accountant's responsibility. They may mean considering incorporation (instead of the traditional partnership arrangement) in states where that provides some protection against liability. And they may involve turning down a client if the engagement appears to entail high risk. As a claims representative for the AICPA's professional liability insurance plan advised an Institute conference in early 1986, high-risk engagements might include audits of financial institutions, construction companies, grain elevators, and manufacturers. "In the last category," according to the *Journal of Accountancy* report on the conference, "two areas of concern are obsolete and nonexistent inventory and bogus accounts receivable." Other high-risk areas are tax practice (accounting for 35 percent of all civil damage suits), management advisory services, and financial services other than audit. In every area, CPAs have been urged to practice defensively. Unfortunately for the rest of us, if they follow this advice to the letter, we may not be able to secure a CPA's services when those services are most needed.

Narrowing the Gap

When it comes to narrowing the expectation gap, there are two divergent approaches. One would rely on external regulators, particularly the SEC and Congress. The other would rely on internal efforts by the accounting profession to regulate itself. (A third proposal—by Big Eight firm Price Waterhouse—to establish a government-supervised self-regulatory organization modeled in part after the National Association of Securities Dealers has received little support. The other seven of the Big Eight, in fact, oppose the idea.)

Which will win out? It's impossible to be certain at this writing, but it is possible that they will converge. It's very possible that successful efforts at self-regulation will eliminate the perceived need for government regulation. Before examining self-regulatory efforts, however, let's see what the government, specifically the Dingell Committee, has in mind.

Government Intervention

When the Securities Acts of 1933 and 1934 were initially passed, the Securities and Exchange Commission was given the statutory authority to set accounting standards. That authority has been left by the SEC in the hands of the private sector. As a result, the Financial Accounting Standards Board sets the standards that the SEC enforces. Why did this happen? Well, according to one account, the SEC's first chief accountant, Carman Blough, argued that the development of accounting principles should be left to the accounting profession because practicing accountants faced accounting and auditing problems on a daily basis and were well equipped to resolve such problems. In April 1938, therefore, by a vote of three to two, the SEC encouraged the acceptance of generally accepted accounting principles, and set the pattern for the relationship between itself and the profession for the next fifty years.

While this relationship generally pleases both the SEC and the accounting profession, it does have its critics. There are people who claim that it makes a mockery of regulatory procedures, since it is the regulated who are in fact setting the standards by which they are regulated. The Metcalf Committee in the mid-1970's virtually accused the SEC of being a puppet of the Big Eight accounting firms, the AICPA, and the Financial Accounting Standards Board. "To an astounding degree," the staff report reads, "the SEC has permitted, and even insisted upon, establishment of accounting standards which have substantial impact on the Federal Government and the public by self-interested private accounting organizations. The result has been an extraordinary delegation of public authority and responsibility to narrow private interests." In response, the SEC notes that the system works well and the public interest is protected. When necessary, in fact, actions of the private sector are overridden; a recent example is in accounting for the oil and gas industries, where the national interest in encouraging exploration overrode a proposed move toward unified accounting standards.

The 1977 Committee's staff report also criticized the SEC for treating large accounting firms more leniently than individual CPAs and small firms in disciplinary actions. The latter have been suspended from practice before the SEC, while the former in similar situations have received mild sanctions. In response, notes SEC chief accountant Clarence Sampson, "If a sole practitioner files a fraudulent statement, we have little choice but to suspend him from his practice because he is the firm. Where a firm has one thousand partners, do you ban the whole firm or just the partner? We look at the quality control system. If the system has broken down, it's the firm's responsibility. If the individual went around the system, it's something else. We can name the individual, the firm, or both. Either way, there is public disclosure of those sanctioned."

Today, the House Subcommittee on Oversight and Investigations of the Committee on Energy and Commerce, in echoes of the 1970's, is reviewing accounting disclosure standards. The Subcommittee, according to staff director Michael F. Barrett, Jr., wants to see how well accounting practices and disclosures have worked since the inception of the SEC. It is concerned about recent bank failures and about scandals in other publicly held companies, some of which are related to accounting practices. "Finally," notes Barrett, "the Subcommittee will review what, if any changes are needed in the laws, their administration, or the regulations promulgated thereunder."

The Subcommittee has been holding hearings for two years at this writing and expects to continue. Meanwhile, in a surprise move in the midst of the hearings, Representative Ron Wyden introduced a bill in the House of Representatives that would require auditors to report suspected fraud or illegal acts to the SEC or other appropriate regulatory bodies. Auditors would also be required to disclose publicly any known or suspected fraudulent activities of a client, but the bill would provide legal protection for auditors making such disclosure "in good faith." The bill would require auditors to examine the internal controls of publicly controlled clients, and to give a written opinion regarding the adequacy of such controls.

In introducing the bill, in May 1986, Representative

Wyden alluded to a number of recent financial "disasters," including E. F. Hutton, United American Bank, Penn Square Bank, E. S. M. Government Securities, Home State Savings and Loan of Ohio—and noted that "the disaster struck virtually on the heels of a stipulation by audit firms that the companies were financially sound. The result? Hundreds of thousands of investors and creditors were out hundreds of millions of dollars. . . . Because the regulators and the profession have abdicated their responsibility, we feel it is time for Congress to step in."

Both the regulators and the profession, however, deny that they have abdicated their responsibility. That responsibility and the ways in which it is carried out have been clearly identified in lengthy testimony before Congress. Speaking for the SEC, for example, chairman John S. R. Shad told the committee that requiring independent auditors to detect and disclose illegal and fraudulent activities as the bill specifies would increase audit fees by three or four times current amounts. Much of what the bill proposes is already being done at the Commission, Shad went on to note, so that there would not be much benefit from its passage. Furthermore, auditors do not have the expertise to identify any and all potentially illegal acts, particularly those outside the financial area. Look at Occupational Health and Safety regulations, for example, or Environmental Protection Agency rules; how could auditors be expected to familiarize themselves with all of these rules and regulations?

More to the point, perhaps, fraud is not and never has been simply overlooked. Any evidence of fraud must, right now, be presented to management. If appropriate action is not taken by management, the auditor must consider resigning the engagement. If indeed the auditor does resign, then a form 8-K must be filed with the SEC; that form, which is publicly disclosed, includes information about client-auditor disagreements. While Wyden criticized this procedure as being ineffective, the SEC points out that the auditors must be reluctant to make charges against a client without proof. The AICPA, meanwhile, has proposed revision of 8-K requirements so that, when an auditor is changed, management would have to report the following:

- Whether, in either of the last two audits, the auditor has communicated concerns regarding management integrity or possible irregularities that were not resolved to the auditor's satisfaction;
- Whether the audit committee or board of directors had discussed the communication with the auditor;
- Whether the auditor has been authorized to respond fully to the inquiries of the successor accountant.

The Wyden bill, in any case, as Shad pointed out, would do nothing to prevent collusive fraud, the kind of situation where many members of management are working together to deceive the auditors. Such instances are rare, but when they do happen they can be virtually impossible to detect.

Perhaps more important, in the eyes of the profession, the original bill had two overriding faults: It omitted a "materiality" standard, under which auditors could only be expected to identify violations of a material nature; without such a standard, auditors might be reduced to counting paper clips. And it failed to recognize that any "whistle-blowing" requirement could impair the relationship between the auditor and the client.

A revised version of the Wyden bill takes account of the criticism and makes some changes. Under this version, auditors would be required to bring possible fraudulent abuses to a corporation's audit committee or board of directors, who would be responsible for reporting to regulatory authorities. If the suspected abuses are not material to the financial statements, then the auditor's obligations under the bill end. If the abuses are material, and if management failed to take action, then the auditors would be required to go to the authorities.

While this version sits better with the accounting profession, it is still not satisfactory. The profession would, of course, prefer no government regulation at all. As Ed Kangas puts it, "Auditors in a free enterprise, capitalistic society should be independent of all outside influences, including government. Otherwise the day could come when a government, to 'prove' that its programs have been successful, starts influencing accounting and auditing rules." But if there is to be regulation, it should be carefully thought out and executed. It should not be, as *Accounting Office Management & Administration Report* characterized the Wyden bill, "a repressive, ill-conceived, and vindictive shotgun blast."

More temperate critics say that the proposed legislation is both unnecessary and unworkable. It's unnecessary because the profession can and does regulate itself, and because the quality of audits in the United States is very high indeed. "We must keep in perspective that the number of cases even *alleging* audit failure in these highly litigious times," Philip Chenok noted in his testimony before the Dingell Committee in June 1986, concerning audits of publicly held companies, "involve only three-tenths of one percent of the audits performed over the last six years." And it's unworkable because the definitions of "illegality" and "irregularity" are vague and nonspecific, because CPAs don't have subpoena power to secure documents from recalcitrant clients, and because they neither can nor should act as policemen.

Self-regulation

The profession itself has taken numerous steps toward maintaining quality control; more action is under way.

Peer review may be one of the most important means of self-regulation. Since the Division for Firms of AICPA was formed in 1977, a requirement for membership in this voluntary program has been regular peer review. Member firms are reviewed every three years, either by another firm or by one of a team of reviewers put together by the Institute or by other authorized bodies. The reviewers go to the firm and assess the quality-control systems and compliance with those systems by studying the design of the systems, inspecting audit workpapers and administrative files, and interviewing personnel, all in an effort to make sure that audits are conducted in accordance with professional standards.

The Public Oversight Board, an independent body, oversees and reviews all peer reviews of member firms in the SEC Practice Section of the Division for Firms. Sometimes the Board's oversight procedures are intensive, involving observation of the review and a look at all the workpapers; some do not entail a visit but do involve intensive review of the workpapers; some are a summary review. The most intensive reviews generally apply to the firms with the most SEC clients. The Securities and Exchange Commission, which endorses this process, has access to the workpapers of the Public Oversight Board. In addition, on a sample basis, the SEC has access to the workpapers of any firm that has an SEC client.

The SEC Practice Section also has a Special Investigations Committee (SIC). A member firm is obligated to report promptly to the SIC any litigation and/or governmental proceedings directed against it alleging deficiencies in the conduct of an audit of an SEC client. In the first seven years of the SIC (1979 to 1986), 203 alleged audit failures were placed on its agenda; 22 were still being considered at the end of 1986. Of the rest, many cases were dismissed because either the allegations misstated the requirements of professional standards or the case did not indicate a need for corrective measures. In 25, however, AICPA technical bodies were asked to consider the need for changes in or additional guidance on professional standards. Eleven were referred to the AICPA Professional Ethics Division with a recommendation for an investigation into the work of specific individuals. In 20 cases a special review was conducted or a regularly scheduled peer review was expanded. And in 24 the firm took appropriate corrective action. Such action included reassignment of personnel, additional supervisory procedures for specific individuals, special continuing professional education programs, and so on.

Much criticism has focused on the secrecy surrounding these procedures. In 1986 the SEC was given limited access to the SIC process; it would like additional access, and the arrangement is under study. The AICPA believes that the names of those who are under investigation by its Ethics Division but who have not yet been found guilty should remain secret. But guilty findings in AICPA disciplinary procedures are published, and peer review results are publicly available.

Meanwhile, criticism of the peer review process, by Congress and others, contends that the result is almost always a whitewash. How could it be anything else, asks Abe Briloff, "when it's 'you scratch my back, I'll scratch yours'?" Where it isn't, critics go on, the only "punishment" is a slap on the wrist. At the root of the matter, however, is the view of punishment. "Government regulation is measured by scalps on the belt," says 1987–88 AICPA chairman Marvin Strait. "Government has to look at punishment in terms of licenses pulled. Self-regulation, on the other hand, aims at improvement of practice. It's designed to rehabilitate, to correct substandard practice."

In fact, firms receive modified or adverse reports about 11 percent of the time, and the process keeps getting tougher. Recent changes in peer review standards include additional minimum qualifications for reviewers; guidelines to enhance uniformity in reporting; a requirement to consider litigation in the selection of offices and engagements for review; and a requirement to report that individual offices are not up to standard, even if a multi-office firm taken as a whole merits a "clean" peer review report.

Other reviews take place on the state level. The National Association of State Boards of Accountancy has a model program of "positive enforcement," under which state boards monitor the performance of licensed accountants. In Nebraska, for instance, the University of Nebraska-Lincoln School of Accounting has started reviewing sample audit reports. In Kentucky teams of management-level accountants, under the aegis of the Kentucky Board of Accountancy, review submitted audit reports and comment on their quality.

Further changes will take place if peer review becomes mandatory. The AICPA's Anderson Committee, in its far-reaching report, proposed a national practice-monitoring program for all AICPA members in public practice. This proposal should come to a vote by the end of 1987. It also proposed that firms with SEC clients be required to join the SEC Practice Section. Although 61 percent of Institute members voted for the latter proposal in spring 1987, this fell short of the required two-thirds majority and the proposal was defeated. The SEC, meanwhile, proposed that CPA firms auditing publicly held companies undergo peer review at least once every three years.

The defeated proposal would have made peer review a condition of Institute membership for CPAs who are partners of firms auditing publicly held companies. Approximately 84 percent of all audits of publicly held companies are currently conducted by firms voluntarily undergoing peer review as members of the AICPA SEC Practice Section. Other firms conducting such audits, if their partners were willing to forgo the benefits of Institute membership, could have continued to audit public companies. The SEC proposal would make peer review a condition of practicing before the Commission, thereby effectively prohibiting nonparticipants in the peer review program from auditing publicly held companies. Peer review, under the SEC proposal, would be conducted by peer review organizations such as the AICPA'S SEC Practice Section. Alternatively, a firm would have the option of a review performed by another firm under SEC supervision.

There are some questions about just how effective mandatory quality review will be. Review teams will probably select the work to be reviewed, as they do now under voluntary peer review. But if practitioners and firms can choose the reports they submit for review, as they now do under some state review programs, they will submit their best work. Will this hide other problems? If reviewers disclose only general statistics about reviews, concealing the identity of specific firms and practitioners, will the public interest be served? And if most substandard audits are found among smaller firms or individual practitioners, as the Brooks Report seems to indicate, will they resent the entire process and consider it discriminatory?

In answer, James T. Ahler, executive director of the Kentucky Board of Accountancy, told the *Louisville Times* that even when people send their best reports, those best reports often don't measure up. "If the guy sends us what he thinks is his best report, and it's still substandard, that's the guy we want to catch." As for disclosure, the process is meant to be educational and not punitive; the public interest will be served if firms bring substandard performance up to par. Public availibility of peer review reports was contemplated under the Anderson Committee proposals, and is considered important by the SEC.

Some small practitioners, particularly those represented by the National Conference of CPA Practitioners (NCCPAP), have long objected to both the AICPA's voluntary peer review program and to the whole idea of mandatory quality review. "It's a burden for the small practitioner," says Maxine K. Young of Young & Company in Fort Wayne, Indiana. "Why single out the small practitioner? Most of them worked for big firms before they started their own practices. And, even more important, the small firms are responsible for what they do. I don't hire green college graduates and send them out on engagements. I can't afford to do that, because what I do represents *me*." (In what appears to be a turnaround, NCCPAP announced in February 1987 that it was developing its own voluntary peer-review program. This program is being designed to satisfy the proposed SEC requirement.)

Analysis of the data in the Brooks Committee report about substandard audits of government programs indicated that smaller firms whose quality controls had not been subject to peer review performed severely substandard work 41 percent of the time, while firms that did have peer review were accused of severe standards violations only 2 percent of the time. Perhaps quality review *is* necessary. And perhaps smaller firms and sole practitioners can adjust to quality review if it is phased in slowly over a period of time. After all, many large firms didn't like the idea of peer review either when it was first suggested. "I spoke of positive enforcement ten years ago at NASBA," says Bob Ellyson, managing partner of Coopers & Lybrand in Miami, "and people thought I was crazy. Then, when I suggested mandatory quality review on the Anderson Committee in late 1983, it wasn't well received. But sentiment has swung rapidly, and now there's a willingness to accept review of practice." One might say that there's more than a willingness among the profession's leaders; there's an urgent feeling, as AICPA chairman J. Michael Cook put it, that "peer review is here to stay." In view of the strong majority of members supporting mandatory peer review, the Institute is supporting the thrust of the SEC proposal.

Auditing standards are another area undergoing revision. Here, as in the realm of accounting standards (although statutory authority is a little fuzzier), the SEC relies on the profession. And the profession is taking action. "We're concerned with trying to narrow the gap," said AICPA audit VP Dan M. Guy, "by better explaining and in certain cases increasing the responsibility to be more in accord with public expectations." Moving in this direction, the Auditing Standards Board of the AICPA is refining and redefining a number of auditing standards. In early 1987 the Board issued exposure drafts revising ten statements on auditing standards.

Although the auditor currently has a clear responsibility to search for errors and irregularities that would be material to the financial statements being examined, as part of the larger responsibility to report on financial statements, there is concern that some auditors do not understand this responsibility. There is also some feeling that the relevant standard does not provide sufficient guidance on how to detect errors and irregularities. The proposed revision attempts to clarify the responsibility and provide the requisite guidance. The emphasis is on professional skepticism. Or, as Auditing Standards Board chairman Jerry Sullivan of Coopers & Lybrand told *The Wall Street Journal*, the new rules "will force the auditor to look under almost every rock."

Another standard under revision concerns auditor communications. The big change here is in the form of the auditor's report. Currently every report's standard language, commonly called boilerplate, consists of two paragraphs, a "scope" paragraph stating what was done and an opinion paragraph communicating what was found. The revised boilerplate ("We've got to stick to standard language," Guy says, "so the language is clear to both CPAs and users") will have three paragraphs. The introductory paragraph will state what financial statements are covered, and will specify that these are the client's financial statements; this is meant to contrast the auditor's role with that of management. Paragraph two will explain the objectives of the audit, making clear the auditor's responsibility for detecting errors or irregularities. Paragraph three will give the auditor's opinion.

Also in the communications realm is a proposed standard on the examination of the management discussion and analysis (MD&A), the information that management of public companies provides about trends, plans, and the like. "This is a very revealing part of a financial statement package. A lot of information about risks and uncertainties is in MD&A," Guy says. "We aren't making it a required service—we can't require an audit in this area—but if a client wants it, we can attest to the MD&A and to its completeness." Some would have this standard go further. Under a proposal made by seven of the Big Eight (in response to Price Waterhouse's proposal for an SRO), management would be required to enhance the relevance of financial statements through improved disclosure of risk and uncertainties. And these disclosures would be subject to audit coverage. Says Duane Kullberg of Arthur Andersen, "We suggested annual disclosure in corporate financial statements of the types of risk that federal law already requires management to disclose in initial securities registrations."

Along these same lines the Institute's Accounting Standards Executive Committee (AcSEC) is proposing ways to improve communication in financial statements so as to help users better assess the risks and uncertainties associated with a business enterprise. Among the proposals, which will probably be considered by the Financial Accounting Standards Board once they are formally recommended by AcSEC, is one that would require companies to disclose risks and uncertainties, specifically those stemming from concentration. A company might be vulnerable, as an example, if it had only one supplier for a crucial part or if it relied on a single major customer for much of its sales volume. This proposal has been scaled down from an earlier version that would have encompassed any risks and uncertainties that might reasonably be expected to have an impact on cash flow or operating results. But it is still highly controversial within the profession because, as with any move away from financial statements as purely historical documents and toward financial statements as forecasts, it casts accountants in the uncomfortable role of prophet.

Another major area under consideration by the Auditing

Standards Board is reporting on a company's system of internal controls. The proposed revision is designed so that auditors will express their responsibilities more clearly with respect to the integrity of these controls. It clarifies the types of deficiencies that should be reported and how the report should be made.

Still another project entails the auditor's responsibility for assessing the continued existence of a client company. A direct offshoot of concern about business failures being audit failures, this proposed standard would require auditors to consider whether there are conditions, cropping up during the audit, indicating a question about the company's continued existence for the following year. Again, says Guy, "We've stepped up our responsibility for viability. We are not forecasting or projecting the continuing existence of the entity, but we are saying that if the evidence indicates a problem with the entity remaining a going concern, then the client is going to have to be forthcoming in disclosing the problem and the problem will be flagged in the auditor's opinion." Or, as Price Waterhouse puts it, "There should be 'early warnings,' in plain English, when a company's financial condition is questionable." With this change, the auditor will have an affirmative responsibility to look at audit documentation from the perspective of whether the entity will remain a going concern—in sharp contrast to today's practice, where the auditor must have a serious question about asset recoverability or liability classification before doing anything.

All of these auditing standards changes have been under consideration for a couple of years. Although they address the concerns of the congressional investigators, therefore, the profession's action predates that investigation. This is more than reflexive reaction. It is, instead, a positive step forward.

So, too, is the work of the National Commission on Fraudulent Financial Reporting. This independent body, established by several national organizations to address this major issue, is chaired by James C. Treadway, Jr., an attorney and former SEC commissioner who is now general counsel of Paine Webber. Its mission, as research director Jack L. Krogstad told *Financial Planning* magazine, is to "examine the relationship between society's ethics and corporate ethics. We hope to ferret out potentially high-risk combinations of individual and corporate pressures that can lead to fraud."

In October 1986, after more than a year of work, Treadway presented the Commission's initial recommendations to the annual convention of the AICPA in Kansas City, Missouri. The recommendations are based on solid research, research which shows:

- Of 456 lawsuits against auditors between 1960 and 1985, management fraud was present in about half of the cases. Only about 20 percent of the bankruptcies studied in the same research revealed litigation against the auditor, disproving the widespread notion that a business failure automatically leads to allegations of audit failure.

- Of 119 actions brought by the SEC against their public companies and 42 actions brought by the SEC against their public auditors since 1980, most alleged frauds were perpetrated by upper-level management via improper revenue recognition or overstatement of assets; most of the alleged frauds occurred because of a breakdown in internal controls; almost a third of the public companies involved in these actions did not have an audit committee; three-quarters of the auditing firms involved were non-national firms, of whom 87 percent were not members of the AICPA's SEC Practice Section and hence not subject to peer review.

- A study sponsored by the National Association of Accountants found no concrete instances where the independence of the public auditor was compromised by the performance by the firm of nonaudit services.

- A study sponsored by the Financial Executives Institute analyzed corporate situations and pressures and found that fraud, rather than being intentional, is frequently the product of a combustible mixture of Board apathy, unrealistic profit pressures, weak controls, and bonus-heavy compensation plans.

After a careful review of these and other studies, the Commission developed preliminary recommendations with respect to reporting entities, to independent auditors, and to regulatory authority. With respect to reporting entities, the Commission suggests:

- Audit Committees should be mandated for all publicly owned corporations, as well as for other entities (such as mutual thrift institutions) that accept public funds. These Audit Committees should include at least a majority of independent directors. "This decision on mandatory Audit Committees," Treadway comments, "reflects our Commission's view that an informed, diligent Audit Committee represents the single most potentially effective influence for minimizing fraudulent financial reporting and that Audit Committees are an integral part of sound internal controls."
- Audit Committees should be activists and should be deeply involved in the financial reporting process. To this end, and because the Commission has found great disparity among Audit Committees' functions and effectiveness, the Commission intends to publish "good practice" guidelines for Audit Committees. Audit Committees, moreover, should be provided adequate resources to discharge their role; that role should be more visible and communicated to the public via a letter in the corporation's annual report.
- Corporate management should be required to express an opinion on the adequacy of internal controls, and should affirmatively acknowledge in the annual report

to stockholders that they have the foremost and ultimate responsibility for accurate financial statements.

- All public companies should have a fraud-risk-assessment and risk-management program. Their internal controls should not be structured mechanically but should emphasize the overall control environment and should be monitored actively by the Audit Committee.

- All public companies should be required to maintain an internal audit function; the Commission will publish "good practice" guidelines related to this function.

- The chief internal auditor should report directly to the chief executive officer or to a senior financial officer who does not have direct involvement in the preparation of the company's financial statements. The chief internal auditor should also have direct access to the Audit Committee and meet privately with that committee on a regular basis.

- Because corporate culture has much to do with the quality of financial reporting, the Commission recommends that all companies adopt, publicize, and enforce written codes of conduct. The Audit Committee should evaluate compliance with the code, on an annual basis, focusing on matters such as perks and the use of company assets.

With respect to independent auditors, the Treadway Commission recommends the following:

- Auditing standards relating to the auditor's responsibility to detect fraud need to be clarified. The Auditing Standards Board, as noted, is already addressing this issue, but the Commission suggests that the ASB be restructured to include public representation and participation. The Commission rejects the approach taken in the Wyden bill because it "would introduce an unworkable adversarial atmosphere into the audit process."

- The standard auditor's report should be revised to better communicate the auditor's role and responsibilities and its inherent limitations. The ASB is also addressing this issue.
- The SEC should mandate membership in a professional quality-assurance program, such as the AICPA SEC Practice Section or its equivalent, for all auditors involved in audits of public companies.
- Independent accountants should be required to conduct a timely review of quarterly financial reports, rather than reserving review for annual reports; these quarterly reports should be accompanied on the corporate side by increased oversight and participation by the Audit Committee.
- The independence of the public auditor should be regularly evaluated by the Audit Committee. The evaluation should consider the extent of nonaudit services provided by the public auditor; the level of audit fees relative to nonaudit fees should be a required disclosure in the Annual Report.
- Greater emphasis should be placed on analytical review procedures, which have proved to be effective in detecting potential fraudulent financial reporting.
- The public auditor should publicly provide a negative assurance opinion on internal controls.

With respect to regulation, Treadway emphasizes the Commission's view that "the SEC must be active, tough-minded, resourceful, and sufficiently funded and staffed." When it comes to penalties and sanctions, the Commissions recommends:

- More severe sanctions, including barring from corporate office "those who cause, aid and abet, or participate in fraudulent financial reporting. . . . We see no basis for treating corporate offenders differently from the auditors when it comes to sanctions."

• More criminal prosecutions and longer sentences for fraudulent financial reporting.

In late April 1987 the Treadway Commission issued its final report for comment. Its recommendations were essentially the same as those described above, with minor modifications. The Treadway Commission marks a thoughtful and intensive effort toward honest financial reporting. Its recommendations, if adopted, together with the self-regulatory efforts of the accounting profession, should go a long way toward restoring public confidence and forestalling any need for government intervention.

7

We, the People: Accounting for Government

"The accounting profession needs to take a much broader interest in what's going on in Washington," says Congressman Joseph J. DioGuardi, one of only four CPAs in Congress. "Fiscal issues are at the top of the heap, and the profession should bring its expertise to the table." DioGuardi has brought *his* expertise to the table, based on twenty-two years in public accounting. With initial plans to become a lawyer transformed by a college internship at Arthur Andersen, DioGuardi is now focusing his efforts on bringing efficient financial management to Washington. "Unless you get into the bowels of government," he insists, "you'll never find the real waste."

From four-hundred-dollar wrenches to multibillion-dollar defense systems, the cost of government is repeatedly questioned. The spenders of the public purse have been accused of everything from careless waste to outright abuse to total disregard of accountability. How many of the accusations are true? It's hard to be sure, but one thing is certain: Government functions by rules of its own. Government does things that the private sector couldn't do, and government accounting is a field in and of itself.

Government accounting (or lack thereof) is a complicated subject. We'll touch here on just two areas: accounting for federal expenditures, and auditing of federal grant recipients.

Accounting for the Costs of Government

"Over the centuries the financing of governments has vied with religion, ethnicity, and territory as a principal object of civil contention, disruption, and war," wrote Frederick C. Mosher in *A Tale of Two Agencies*, his insightful examination of the General Accounting Office and the Office of Management and Budget. The fight over taxation—remember the Boston Tea Party?—was a principal cause of the American Revolution. Today disputes over attempts to reduce the budget deficit divide lawmakers and may ultimately arouse the public.

Despite the enormous concern over government financial affairs, however, government accounting is something else. Things haven't gotten much better—in fact, many observers believe they've gotten worse—since Thomas Jefferson commented, in 1802, "I think it an object of great importance . . . to simplify our system of finance, and to bring it within the comprehension of every member of Congress . . . the whole system [has been] involved in impenetrable fog . . . we might hope to see the finances of the Union as clear and intelligible as a merchant's books, so that every member of Congress, and every man of any mind in the Union, should be able to comprehend them to investigate abuses, and consequently to control them."

The situation may have deteriorated in just the last couple of years. The President's Private Sector Survey on Cost Control (the Grace Commission) reported in 1983 that there were 332 separate federal accounting systems, of which 123, or 37 percent, were not approved by the General Accounting Office as required by law. In 1986, the GAO reported that the federal government was up to 427 separate accounting systems, of which 226, or 53 percent, were not approved.

The almost incomprehensible rate of growth of the federal government has contributed to the problem. As *The*

Government Accountants Journal has noted, "In the early 1960's the federal budget was a mere $60 billion and there were only a few hundred governmental programs." Twenty years later, the federal government is enormous, with a budget exceeding a trillion dollars. It has "2,000 different federal programs administered by over 150 departments, agencies and offices, at some 25,000 locations, [with] 2,500,000 civilian workers occupying 400,000 buildings."

With this growth, a recent report of the General Accounting Office found, "Federal finances are managed through an elaborate structure of decision processes and information systems. Many of these processes and systems, now obsolete, face ever-increasing difficulties in coping with the demands placed upon them." The difficulties crop up in the annual fight over the budget, in the cumbersome and time-consuming decision-making process, in ineffective controls over how federal money is spent, and in budgeting, accounting, and management information systems that too often yield data that the comptroller general himself has called unreliable, inconsistent, and even irrelevant.

The Grace Commission, dismayed at the chaos stemming from the lack of government accountability, raised a number of alarming questions:

- Does the government know how much it is owed? Apparently not. When a collection program was finally launched, it took a special group in OMB eighteen months to determine how much the government was owed in outstanding loans (guaranteed student loans are just one example), tax delinquencies, and the like.
- Can the government keep track of its property? Also, apparently not. The Department of Defense, as just one example, maintains inadequate controls over material furnished to contractors.
- Can the federal government keep track of expenditures? Again, the answer seems to be no, at least in

part because cost information is generally not processed and maintained by function.

• Can the government even keep track of its own systems? With 427 separate and distinct accounting systems, many of them operating on rules of their own, the answer, once again, appears to be no.

The problems are extensive. The comptroller general's report points to five major areas:

1. Lack of cost information. With floods of information pouring out of the federal government, there is still little of the reliable cost data essential for effectively monitoring current programs and providing a basis for future program and budget planning.

2. Lack of reliable information on weapon systems. Current project reporting systems in this major area of government spending are not tied to the accounting and budgeting systems. Congress and the executive branch lack the information necessary to see a particular project's expected cost and how that cost compares to previous estimates; no one can see exactly how much money has been spent and on what.

3. Inadequate disclosures of costs and liabilities. Major commitments of federal resources, such as future pension benefits, are only partially recognized in the budget. Other activities—and the report specifically mentions the $106.9 billion loan portfolio of the Federal Financing Bank—are completely omitted from budget totals. (Actually over $350 billion in government accounts and loan receivables escape all notice in cash basis accounts.)

4. Unstructured planning for capital investment. Vitally important decisions about capital investment are made in an uncoordinated fashion; the government's overall approach to capital budgeting gives capital expenditures little visibility in the budget process. Well over $100 billion a year is spent on capital assets and physical infrastructure that will provide benefits over a period of many years;

current government accounting treats these capital outlays as a current cost of operations.

5. Antiquated financial management systems. The federal government, the report points out, is the largest and most complex operating organization in the world. Yet its basic approach to financial management is both obsolete and inefficient. Many federal systems employ outdated equipment. ("The government has about nineteen thousand computers," notes Connor of Price Waterhouse, co-chairman of the Grace Commission's Task Force on Federal Management Systems, "many of them so outdated they are no longer serviced by the companies that manufactured them.") Moreover, the systems themselves are not designed to provide the information needed by managers, policy officials, and Congress.

Efforts have been made over the years to strengthen federal financial management. Yet the efforts have been, by and large, piecemeal. There is no one coordinating agency in overall charge of federal financial management. Each department and each agency handles its own financial affairs. Each department has its own undersecretary for financial management (and the average tenure is just eighteen months, according to a report by the National Academy of Public Administrators, strongly suggesting a lack of continuity). Most departments, but not all, have inspectors general in charge of investigations and audits. Put another way, no one is minding the store. "There is," notes Robert L. Shultis, former executive director of the National Association of Accountants, "no person or group of people with overall financial responsibility to help run a trillion-dollar-a-year business!"

As just one egregious example: The approximately one hundred payroll systems currently in use in federal agencies are incompatible. "Inconsistent procedures," says Joe Connor, "are applied to record similar transactions." The overall costs of these payroll systems range from $500,000 to $32,000,000. Or, in down-to-earth terms, the cost of issuing a federal payroll check currently varies from about $2 to about $14 depending on which payroll system is used.

Every department and agency may seem to go its own way but financial authority is, at least on paper, somewhat concentrated. The three principal financial agencies in the federal government are the Department of the Treasury, the Office of Management and Budget (OMB), and the General Accounting Office. The first two are arms of the executive branch. As such Treasury is concerned primarily with inflow-outflow of funds, and the government's cash position; OMB, while "Management" is its middle name, is concerned primarily with formulating budgets. The General Accounting Office is an arm of the legislative branch, concerned among other things with the overseeing of government spending.

While these three agencies are nominally in charge, the Grace Commission's Task Force on Federal Management Systems concluded that the real problem is a "missing link" in the federal government's financial management structure. "That is," wrote Joe Connor, "no single organization bears responsibility for directing or carrying out the government's financial management functions." The result, says a 1985 editorial in *The Government Accountants Journal*, "ultimately leads to confusion and ample opportunity to 'pass the buck.'"

Accounting Methods and Madness

While the government does have an internal auditor, in the form of the GAO, it appears to lack the function of an accountant. What's more, it lacks financial statements (required in the private sector) that would permit objective evaluation of government policies and programs.

There are problems with both budgeting and financial reporting. While budgeting is not strictly an accounting concern, budgeting and accounting, as Connor put it in testimony before the Senate Committee on Governmental Affairs, "are inexorably intertwined. The former deals with planning for fiscal expenditures and the latter the reporting of the actual results of those plans."

On the budget front, the federal government does not separate capital and operational budgets. Proposals have been made to separate the federal budget into two parts: an operating budget (akin to a profit-and-loss statement in the private sector) and a capital budget (like a balance sheet). Cash outlays on capital investments would show up on the capital budget; upkeep of those investments would appear on the operating budget. Proponents say that a two-part budget could bring capital spending under control and help the government plan for future costs of maintenance and repair. Opponents fear that the process would be subject to excessive political pressure. "The clear incentive for the proponents of each spending program," Gregory J. Ballantine of Peat Marwick Mitchell & Co. wrote in *The Wall Street Journal*, "would be to have their program classified as a capital outlay so that it would not have to be paid for by current taxes and would not count against the deficit."

The same kind of challenge shows up in the area of financial reporting. There are three ways in which economic events may be measured: on an obligation basis, a cash basis, or an accrual basis. Generally, the obligation basis measures the resources officially committed to carry out government programs. Obligations occur when orders are placed or contracts awarded. Obligation-based reporting does not provide a complete picture and can, in fact, indicate distorted information. Congress may budget $1 billion for a Navy ship in a single year, for example, yet no funds may actually be expended for the ship in that year.

The cash basis measures current cash inflow and outflow, with results computed as the difference between cash received and cash disbursed. On a cash basis, expenditures for the ship would be recorded when paid. This, too, can be misleading because inventory purchased in one year and consumed in the following year would be reflected in the first year's operations. Cash-basis information is critical for effective cash management, but it is inadequate as a complete measure because it does not consider when revenues are earned or costs incurred, making it impossible to evaluate the annual cost of programs or the annual results of operations.

On an accrual basis the effect of financial transactions is recognized as they occur rather than when obligations are incurred or when cash is received or paid. Revenues are recognized when earned, assets when acquired, and costs when resources are consumed. Under accrual-based accounting, for example, pension benefits are recognized when they are earned.

All three methods of accounting are important; all provide different but complementary information. Currently, however, the federal government keeps its books on a cash basis (Congressman DioGuardi, who wants to change the system, calls it "Mickey Mouse" accounting), while ignoring accrual accounting. A well-run business, critics argue, can't ignore accrual accounting if it is going to monitor its financial position and the use of available resources. Neither can a well-run government. "Applying this logic to our personal lives," according to Comptroller General Charles Bowsher, "would argue that [you] write off the full cost of building a house in the year you build it."

Under cash-based accounting, future obligations in the form of incurred liabilities don't exist. Cash-basis measures do not include contractual commitments for purchases and programs where future expenditures will be required. "In the defense area alone," Bowsher wrote to Senator William Proxmire in July 1986, "hundreds of billions of dollars are committed for military hardware under firm contracts which will require future outlays.

However, those amounts are not disclosed in our current cash basis deficit reporting."

The result bears no resemblance to sound accounting practice. "Currently, attention is focused solely on the obligation and cash information needed to control appropriations and calculate the deficit," Bowsher wrote. "This approach serves valid cash management and fiscal needs, but it leaves out important information about the long-term costs of government." Accrual-based calculations would provide this cost data, and would provide solid information about the federal government's overall financial condition. Making the change, of course, might have temporarily adverse effects. If the government did keep its books in accordance with generally accepted accounting principles, the budget deficit could be considerably larger than its present staggering total. In fiscal year 1984, for example, cash basis accounting yielded a deficit of $185 billion; accrual basis accounting, according to Treasury Department prototype consolidated financial statements, produced a figure of $215 billion. Estimates by Arthur Andersen & Co., which recognize the Social Security system's unfunded liability, bring the 1984 deficit up to $333 billion.

Some folks think the federal government should change its ways. Among those lined up in favor of change: Comptroller General Charles Bowsher, the Association of Government Accountants, several major CPA firms. Many think the need is urgent. As Duane Kullberg, managing partner of Arthur Andersen, puts it: "Fiscal crises often stem from a lack of accountability, inadequate or misleading financial information, and a failure to account properly for the full cost of long-term programs." Such fiscal crises beset several major cities, New York City among them, in the mid-1970's. Oddly enough, the federal government at that time recognized both the problem and the cure. Kullberg goes on, in a viewpoint he wrote for *Fortune*: "In return for the emergency assistance it provided to New York City, the Treasury ordered the city to convert to accrual accounting for financial reporting and budgeting, and to undergo annual audits." This was a major step forward for state and local governments because, as Charles Bowsher puts it, "The New York City fiscal crisis was to the public sector what the crash of 1929 was to the private sector. People realized they had to get their financial reporting systems in order." Yet where the federal government used to put local governments to shame in accounting practices, today the reverse is true. The federal government has yet to put its own house in order. Many think the time is ripe.

Others disagree. "As a general rule," John T. Crehan, retired director of accounting policy in the Office of the Secretary of Defense, wrote in *The Government Accountants Journal*, "I found that those opposed to the use of general purpose financial statements were from the 'budget' side of the house, or were appropriation-oriented accountants. Those in favor were management accounting types, brought up on the teachings of modern day accounting professors who stress utilization of accounting data in making management decisions." This may be a generalization, but it does seem to be true that the budget people, who must deal with specific planned expenditures, see little value in general purpose financial statements. These nay-sayers may be right in one regard: a total changeover of accounting procedures would be both costly and difficult.

But the voices of change are gathering force and may prevail. Federal agencies have been told to start preparing accrual-based financial reports. (In fact, federal law for many years has required accrual accounting but, since there are no penalties for failing to comply, the law has simply been ignored.) The Treasury itself prepares an unofficial consolidated financial statement. The Office of the Auditor General of Canada and the United States General Accounting Office have joined forces to produce a model government financial statement.

New Ways

Just what change is needed? The comptroller general's 1985 report describes proper financial management process as beginning with planning and programming and running through budget formulation and presentation, budget execution and accounting, and the audit/evaluation phase. In the planning and programming phase, objectives are formulated and a program designed to achieve those objectives. Budgeting establishes the level of resources needed to reach the objectives and sets policy for conducting the work. Budget execution and accounting works out the plan and monitors compliance. Auditing confirms the accuracy and reliability of financial information, while evaluation provides information about the efficiency of operations and the effectiveness with which programs are achieving their intended objectives. Reliable financial information is a key ingredient to successful evaluations. Right now, however, "The major weakness of the present financial management process lies in the very foundation upon which the overall process is dependent—sound financial information and feedback on results."

The GAO report then highlights four key elements of reform:

1. Strengthened accounting, auditing, and reporting. Government financial systems must be designed to produce complete, reliable, consistent, and timely information.

2. Improved planning and programming. A modern financial management system should include a structured process for considering pressing national issues on both a short-term and long-term basis, identifying alternative courses of action and analyzing their probable future consequences. The process must ensure that the alternatives are accurately and completely costed on the basis of data from integrated accounting systems.

3. Streamlined budget process. Unnecessary repetition, detail, and obstacles to action must be eliminated so that

the federal budget process is made more manageable and is integrated with the planning, programming and accounting phases of financial management. This will entail reform in both the Congress and the executive branch.

4. Systematic measurement of performance. The government needs an integrated and disciplined financial management system providing consistent data on both cost and performance. This is the only way to assess the efficiency and effectiveness of government operations.

Government procedures should include a structured planning process for evaluating and choosing alternatives to achieve desired objectives; resource allocation decisions made within a unified budget; budgeting and accounting on the same basis; the use of accounting principles which match the delivery of services with the cost of the services; financial accountability; the measurement of output as well as input, on a system of performance measurement; and the preparation of consolidated reports.

One of those consolidated reports could be an annual financial report on a government-wide basis. The Federal Government Reporting Study, a joint project of the Office of the Auditor General of Canada and the United States General Accounting Office, studied user need to determine what federal financial information should be reported. Right now government financial reports concentrate primarily on compliance with specific legislation and authorizations. This is important, and must be continued. But compliance reporting isn't enough. "Events of the last few years, particularly the rising and seemingly uncontrollable federal deficits and the financial crises in major cities and states," says the hypothetical president in the illustrative annual financial report prepared in the joint study, "point to the need for a new perspective—one that looks at a government as a total financial entity and describes its financial condition in plain language and plain accounting." A streamlined comprehensive consolidated financial report could help legislators, government planners, economists, corporate users, the media, and ordinary citizens understand the workings of government.

The joint study, although it recommends a summary level financial report, doesn't answer all questions. Federal accounting is complex, to say the least, and further research is required on several major technical issues. For example: How should fixed assets (such as Yellowstone National Park) be defined, valued, and depreciated? Should the financial statements of the central banking system be consolidated with those of the federal government? How should Social Security be reported?

Despite the inconclusive nature of the report in these areas, virtually all users expressed a need for a concise summary annual financial report. Such a report would bring together in an easily read and understood format a consistent set of basic data about the federal government to:

- Give an overview of the financial position and operating results of the entire government;
- Provide a common framework to enhance understanding of government operations;
- Provide a common data base for analysis and for developing and debating policy positions;
- Provide a historical perspective from which to consider future budget and spending proposals;
- Assist users in demanding an accountability for actual results by comparison with earlier projections or budget;
- Facilitate the communication of information about government.

It may be a sad commentary that government currently does not provide this information. Yet it's understandable when you think about the size of the federal government and of how it has developed over the past two hundred years. Some of the surveyed users in the United States, in fact, supported the concept of an annual financial report but did not believe that the government could prepare such a report containing information consistent with other government financial documents because the current accounting systems are not fully integrated. It remains to be seen.

Legislative efforts are under way, meanwhile, that may help to break the information and accountability logjam. Three measures were introduced in 1986.

On the Senate side, Senator William V. Roth, Jr., introduced a bill, the Federal Management Reorganization and Cost Control Act of 1986, that would establish an Office of Financial Management in the Office of Management and Budget. The bill goes beyond pure financial management to include the federal credit system, subsidies, collection procedures, and so on. It places control in the OMB, with the director of OMB designated as the chief financial officer.

In the House, Congressman E. Clay Shaw, Jr., introduced a measure to create a Federal Accounting Practices Review Commission to study, design, and recommend a uniform financial management and accounting system for the federal government.

And Representative DioGuardi introduced a bill, the Federal Financial Management Improvement Act, that would establish a chief financial officer of the United States. This CFO would be appointed by the President for a fixed ten-year term (the CFO could not be fired and could not be reappointed) and would serve in the executive office of the President. The bill also provides for an assistant secretary for financial management in each executive department, a controller in each executive agency, and a Federal Finance Council. In order to cut the deficit, DioGuardi says, we can raise taxes, cut spending, or improve the management of resources already at our disposal. A CFO would function as an "independent quarterback" to pull everything together. "We talk about four-hundred-dollar wrenches, but the problem is systemic and structural. Financial discipline is sorely needed in Washington."

The DioGuardi bill has garnered considerable support.

Price Waterhouse, which first proposed the creation of a chief financial officer for the federal government in 1981, strongly supports the proposal. Partner Gilbert Simonetti, Jr., says, "The bill represents the type of structural change in financial management of the executive branch essential to move into an effective mode. Right now no one is in charge." Comptroller General Bowsher wholeheartedly endorses the concept of a CFO, saying, "The current fragmentation of financial management policy-setting authorization among a number of central management agencies has resulted in redundant, overlapping, and conflicting responsibilities. . . . An independent chief financial officer would provide the needed focus." He also believes that the CFO should be completely independent rather than in OMB.

Auditing Government Expenditures

The subject of intensive criticism for its accounting practices, the federal government has done somewhat better on the audit front, where the General Accounting Office oversees the work of federal agencies in monitoring their own spending. But federal funds, these days, reach much farther afield. Currently, over $100 billion is distributed each year to state and local governments in the form of federal financial assistance. These funds are audited either by internal staff auditors or, very often, by independent CPAs hired by the government entity.

The quality of audits of federal financial assistance funds performed by certified public accountants has recently been under attack. The AICPA found problems relating to professional standards in nearly half of two hundred reports it studied between 1979 and 1984. As mentioned earlier, the Brooks Committee reported in 1986 that an estimated *34 percent* (emphasis in the original) of CPA audits of federal financial assistance funds fail to meet generally accepted government auditing standards. This experience is borne out on the local level. In New York City, where the Human Resources Administration uses approximately one hundred independent CPA firms at any one time to audit its myriad programs, twenty-five to thirty have been suspended or removed from the approved list in the last five years. "Many firms are extremely dedicated," according to Arlene J. Lurie, HRA's deputy administrator of audit services, "but some, big firms and small, do substandard work. One major firm, which has done good work for us, assigned inexperienced people to one audit, with a partner in charge who had no knowledge of government requirements. Quality control was simply not in place, and we're negotiating a settlement on the audit fee that was paid."

Who wants to perform governmental audits, hemmed in as they inevitably are by bureaucratic regulation and competitive bidding? Everyone, it seems, from the largest firms to the not-so-large. There are reasons of prestige, being able to say that you audit a major city or program. There are reasons of profit; money may be lost in the first year of an audit, but future years, it is hoped, will be profitable. There's also an element of public service.

From time to time a governmental audit will reveal skeletons in an administrative closet. The North Slope Borough of Alaska is still under investigation by a federal grand jury, at this writing, after KMG Main Hurdman discovered questionable transactions and possible kickbacks in an audit commissioned by a new borough administration.

At other times, and apparently all too often, audits themselves are deficient. Studies by the General Accounting Office, which formed the basis of the Brooks Report, contain numerous examples of deficient audits, ranging from an educational institution in New York State to a city housing authority in Tennessee to a state health agency in

Utah. Usually deficiencies amount to inadequate documentation of work performed. Sometimes they are more serious. In one egregious example, a CPA firm hired to audit a Colorado Head Start grant hired the program's bookkeeper to assist in the audit. In addition to noting the lack of independence inherent in this procedure, the regional inspector general noted that no internal control work was performed; the CPA countered that there was no need to test the system of internal controls since he had personally designed and implemented the system.

In general, however, substandard audits stem from similar causes. As outlined in the Brooks Report, the underlying reasons include:

1. Unfamiliarity with governmental auditing. Government has rules and regulations not present in the private sector. As a result, government audits must include not only an opinion on the fair presentation of financial statements but testing of compliance with laws and an evaluation of internal controls.

2. Failure to understand the dual client relationship in governmental auditing. The auditor may be hired by the grant recipient, but ultimate responsibility must be to the federal government which is providing the funds. This puts the auditor in a difficult position, but it is a relationship that must be understood.

3. Lax attitude toward governmental auditing. Most firms approach government work in a professional manner. A few, perhaps conscious that CPAs are seldom sued for deficient government audits and therefore do not incur financial liability for substandard government work, do not.

4. Inadequate disciplinary procedures. Self-regulation by the profession itself, in the form of the AICPA, and by the state boards of accountancy, is considered inadequate by the committee.

5. Weak audit procurement procedures. In the government arena, auditors may be chosen by competitive bid-

ding, with the lowest bid taking precedence over quality considerations.

The Brooks Committee notwithstanding, considerable progress has been made in improving the quality of government audits. That progress involves efforts by a number of agencies and organizations.

Improving the Quality of Government Audits

The AICPA sets auditing standards and issues Industry Audit Guides. The General Accounting Office produces manuals outlining Generally Accepted Government Auditing Standards (GAGAS), incorporating AICPA standards, which provide guidance for auditors. There are separate manuals for internal auditing of federal agencies, for the auditing of government programs and activities, and for auditing federally assisted programs.

The GAO manual containing "Standards for Auditing of Governmental Organizations, Programs, Activities and Functions" must be followed in audits of federal funds and is recommended for audits of state and local funds. This "yellow book," used in the audits of most states and municipalities, describes standards for an expanded scope of audit to help ensure full accountability and assist government officials and employees in carrying out their responsibilities. Expanded-scope auditing goes beyond standard auditing and is not intended to be used routinely. In its expansion of the auditor's function, it has three elements; one, two, or all three may be used in any one audit of a government entity:

1. Financial and compliance—to determine (a) whether the financial statements of an audited entity present fairly the financial position and the results of financial operations in accordance with generally accepted accounting principles, and (b) whether the entity has complied with laws and regulations that may have a material effect upon the financial statements.

2. Economy and efficiency—to determine (a) whether the entity is managing and utilizing its resources (such as personnel and property) economically and efficiently, (b) the causes of any inefficiences or uneconomical practices, and (c) whether the entity has complied with laws and regulations concerning matters of economy and efficiency.

3. Program results—to determine (a) whether the desired results or benefits established are being achieved, and (b) whether the agency has considered alternatives that might yield desired results at a lower cost.

The Single Audit Act of 1984

Even while following GAGAS, agencies usually confined their audits to records relating to their own programs, ignoring other federal programs administered by the same recipients. The result: duplication, overlap, underauditing, and overauditing. Or, as Jack Adair of GAO puts it, "I could be at the state or local level, running a program with funds from five or six different federal agencies. Three of those grants to me might never be audited by anybody; the other three might be audited by GAO, state auditors, and local auditors."

Throughout the 1970's, as federal financial assistance grew, federal agencies tended to be concerned only with proper disposition of the specific funds for which they were responsible. The detailed monitoring of each individual program wound up producing, throughout the 1960's and 1970's, what has been called, "tons of data, ounces of information." Program managers did their own thing when it came to collecting data, and the actual data were often merely filed and not used in any constructive way.

Because audit requirements for federal grants were satisfied by separate audit examination of each individual grant, different auditors wound up examining different aspects of the same control system and separate portions of the same records, but no one examined either all the grants or the entire fund recipient at one time. Dissatisfaction with this state of affairs led to a vital legislative measure: the Single Audit Act of 1984. The single-audit concept, put into effect first by an Office of Management and Budget ruling and then by legislation, requires a single audit of all the funds provided to one entity even if those funds are provided under multiple grants. The intent is efficient financial management.

But implementation can be a problem. The governmental entity must provide general purpose financial statements, a schedule of all grants and awards, a schedule of subgrants and subgrantees, and documentation of the grant agreement, terms, and budget. The scope of the audit is, of necessity, extensive. A typical community with a budget of $20 million and a number of federal grants could require several thousand hours of professional time to complete the initial single audit, according to KMG Main Hurdman; that could mean a team of three to five accountants working full-time for several months.

This has significant implications for public accounting firms as well as for local governments. Traditionally, smaller firms have been involved in audits of individual grants. Minority firms, in particular, have found opportunities in the governmental sector. Auditing multiple grants to a single entity requires major resources; this could limit participants in governmental audits to the larger firms.

Under the Single Audit Act of 1984, all state and local governments receiving $100,000 or more of federal funds in any one year must conduct a single audit. Governments receiving funds between $25,000 and $100,000 have the option of conducting a single audit.

The single audit follows GAGAS and expands on traditional financial statement audits. It requires an auditor's statement about the presence of internal control systems designed to provide assurance that federal funds are properly managed and properly distributed. And it requires an auditor's statement that administration of the funds complies with grant requirements.

Is the Single Audit Act leading to better financial management, improved programs, a more efficient use of taxpayer funds? It's too soon to say. The Act is still new—New York City, for example, performed its first single audit for the fiscal year ending June 30, 1986—and many CPAs need additional education on government compliance requirements in order to perform these audits properly.

Audit Reviews

Large governmental entities—New York City is one example—conduct desk reviews of all their audits. Smaller entities may not have the resources to do so. Both large and small governmental units, however, have copies of their audits reviewed by regional inspectors general. In addition, notes Arlene Lurie, "The IGs assist us in providing technical support for conducting the single audit, and in determining the scope of the audit."

The IG concept is relatively new, dating from a 1978 law authorizing inspectors general, with investigative and audit functions, in executive agencies of the federal government. These statutory inspectors general, currently in seventeen federal departments and agencies, oversee both internal spending and the spending of grant recipients. They assist state and local governments in providing technical support for conducting the single audit.

Internally, inspectors general examine funds spent by the federal government and funds due to the federal government. For example: June Brown, now vice-president for finance and administration at Systems Development Corporation, was the first inspector general at the Department of the Interior. She reports, "Interior has responsibility for collecting the government's share of royalty payments for minerals that are mined on public land. In the first six audits, the first six ever done of gas being mined on the continental shelf, we collected $10.6 million in underpayments."

Externally, inspectors general examine funds flowing to grant recipients. Those recipients, as we've seen, are numerous. For example, James B. Thomas, Jr., inspector general in the Department of Education, "deals with about forty-four thousand organizational entities—sixteen thousand school districts, six thousand colleges and universities, ten or eleven thousand lending institutions involved with student loans, plus large numbers of state education agencies, state library commissions, and state rehabilitation centers."

Right from the start, the inspector general program achieved notable savings. At NASA, for instance, auditors questioned over $350 million worth of work completed in 1979, for a net savings of about $50.7 million. In 1979, too, the Department of Health, Education and Welfare reported inspector general-generated cost savings of $1.1 billion. In the same year internal audits recovered $6.2 million at the Department of Housing and Urban Development.

In addition to monitoring the work of government auditors, as noted, the inspectors general monitor the work of nongovernmental auditors involved with government funds. Every audit is subject to a desk review; a certain percentage get a workpaper review as well. "Every time we get a report, and in our agency it's about thirty-five hundred a year," says Jim Thomas, "we do a desk review of that report. About five percent then get a workpaper review. Based on these two kinds of review, we reject or have modified about one out of four." This one-out-of-four rejection rate meshes with the GAO's findings in its 1985 study.

CPAs doing substandard audits are subject to disciplinary action. In a typical instance, an inspector general found that a CPA had made statements in the audit report with no backup support for it in the work papers. The IG referred this particular case to the state board of accountancy in Ohio, and the state board took fourfold action: The CPA involved was required to take forty hours of specific accounting and auditing-related courses during 1986; had to pass a quiz developed by the state board based on the GAO manual; had to sit for the auditing portion of the CPA exam and be notified of successful completion before he could render any opinions on any financial statements in the future, and was fined five hundred dollars, four hundred dollars of which was to be waived once he completed the first three actions.

In the States

In addition to being involved in disciplinary action when cases are referred to them, state boards of accountancy have embarked on a program of positive enforcement under which audits are monitored for adherence to quality. This program of positive enforcement, described in Chapter 6, is currently in force in fourteen states and applies to governmental as well as private-sector audits. Some state societies have similar programs. The Illinois CPA Society, for example, has a mandatory positive enforcement program in the governmental reporting area. "We review financial statements on governmental agencies in the state for quality," says Executive Director Martin Rosenberg, "and deal with seriously substandard reports as matters of professional ethics."

In a step beyond positive enforcement, the Colorado Society of CPAs, via its National Accreditation Board for CPA Specialties, has compiled guidelines for CPAs wishing to become accredited governmental auditing specialists. Under the program, effective in 1987, applicants must have at least three years of experience as a CPA with at least 250 hours per year in specific client governmental audit activities. Experience, at the "in-charge" level of responsibility, must include the single audit, compliance, auditors' reports, etc. The experience requirement is to be substantiated by six references, of which at least three must be from separate current governmental clients. The applicant must pass a six-hour exam. And, once accredited, CPAs must participate in quality review.

Organizational Initiative

The AICPA publishes an audit and accounting guide, which has been updated to incorporate the Single Audit Act of 1984. The Institute also has a voluntary peer review program under the Division for CPA Firms, as noted earlier, and has proposed a mandatory peer review program for all members. And it has procedures under which conductors of substandard audits can be subject to disciplinary action.

In line with its usual emphasis on remediation rather than punishment, the Institute has also proposed a program specifically designed to improve the quality of audits of recipients of federal financial assistance. The program, summarized as the five "E's" includes:

1. Education. Standardized training in governmental accounting and auditing should be mandatory for persons performing governmental audits. In addition, steps should be taken by the AICPA, the regional offices of inspectors general, and state audit oversight organizations to improve the quality of guidance provided.
2. Engagement. The auditor has the ultimate responsibility for meeting professional standards. In order to assist the auditor in fulfilling that responsibility, the process by which auditors are engaged to perform an audit should be improved to ensure that the auditor knows exactly what is expected and necessary. One step toward improvement would have the federal government consolidate its numerous rules for the conduct of single audits. Another would have an office of

inspector general or a state or local audit oversight organization establish and monitor policies and requirements for all government audits.

3. Evaluation. Feedback both enables auditors to correct substandard performance and identifies common problems. Audit evaluation, therefore, should include mandatory peer review, positive enforcement programs by state boards, and evaluation by inspectors general to identify frequently occurring problems and develop solutions.

4. Enforcement. A simpler, more efficient, and more effective disciplinary mechanism should be established by the AICPA, the state societies, and the state boards of accountancy. Guidelines to the process should be developed and distributed to government officials. The status and disposition of referrals of alleged substandard work should be reported to appropriate officials, and auditors should waive their right to confidentiality, if necessary, in order to permit these reports.

5. Exchange of information. Because airing problems and solutions can be helpful, the organizations dealing with government audits should broaden their membership. National and regional intergovernmental audit forums, currently restricted to governmental representatives, should include CPAs in public practice, while AICPA governing bodies and committees should include individuals from the government audit community. Federal, state, and local auditors should also be involved as both teachers and students in the AICPA's governmental accounting and auditing training programs.

Some of these recommendations are already in the process of being implemented and a steering committee, composed of representatives of a number of organizations, is working toward implementing the balance. For starters, the Auditing Standards Board is considering guidance on compliance with laws and regulations. Specific continuing education programs in governmental audit are being developed and expanded. The GAO is currently studying procurement practices and will be issuing a step-by-step procurement handbook because, as Leslie Aronowitz of GAO puts it, "The manner of procurement says something about the quality you get." Proper procurement practices, in other words, may eliminate pervasive underbidding and subsequent shortcuts in the work itself.

The large number of substandard audits of federal grant recipients, like the accusation that business failure is related to audit failure, raises the specter of government regulation. Government, of course, is and should be concerned with monitoring the way its funds are spent. But there are two factors indicating forbearance on the regulatory front. First, it's too soon to judge the effectiveness of the Single Audit Act of 1984. Second, the proposals of the AICPA should be given a chance to work. Increased education in the ins and outs of governmental auditing plus mandatory quality review and adequate disciplinary measures should go a long way toward raising and ensuring the quality of governmental audits.

8

A Global Economy and Technological Change

"The interrelationship of the economy is beyond doubt," says Campbell E. Corfe, director for international services for KMG Main Hurdman in the United States. The internationalization of business is growing rapidly. "It's no longer a question just for the Fortune 500, for General Motors or Union Carbide; it's a question for the three to four million Subchapter S corporations in this country, for the ordinary U.S. businessman who is now thinking a lot more internationally but who is confused and who wants his accountant to give business advice—the tax implications of offshore manufacturing or selling operations; licensing agreements; technology transfers; raising money . . ."

The world is changing in many ways, ways that affect the conduct of business and the practice of accounting. International and multinational businesses flourish. Capital flows from one nation to another, almost without regard to boundaries, as we move toward a global economy. Technology is also flourishing, both making the global economy a reality and changing the ways in which it operates. Telecommunications, computer networks, expert systems, artificial intelligence, technologies already developed and those on the brink of development link companies and subsidiaries, clients and CPAs, investors and stock exchanges, country and country. Above it all hovers the move toward an information economy, a knowledge-based economy in which accountants, the "guardians of records and the determiners of value," in the words of futurist David Pearce Snyder, will flourish.

In order to flourish, however, accountants must change with the changing times. "The orderly organization of information and its effective use for decision-making is basically what accounting is all about," Snyder told an AICPA Symposium on the Future in late 1986. "By establishing and enforcing standardized definitions and practices in financial record-keeping and reporting, accountants assure the quality and comparability of information that is crucial to the collective ability to make sound decisions in every aspect of economic life." In times of relatively little change, executives and investors can base decisions on their own past experience, backed by their accountants' expertise. During periods of rapid change and widespread innovation, however, prior experience—by definition—is a poor guide for decision-making. Under such circumstances, says Snyder, accountants and other advisers become valuable for more than backup; they are looked to for guidance. In turn, those advisers "must re-assess the benchmark definitions and processes upon which they base their judgments."

As business moves into a new era, in short, accounting and accountants cannot lag behind. CPAs must learn to cope with the new era so that they can retain their special role as advisers to business. They must embrace the new technologies, becoming comfortable with them and putting them to use. They must reevaluate the traditional services that accounting provides, and assess those services in terms of changing client needs. They must change firm structure and personnel roles, if necessary, to mesh with new technologies and new services. And they must prepare, more than ever before, to function in a global economy.

Technological Change

"Electronic technology lies at the heart of the emerging 'postindustrial' or 'information' society of today," says Marvin J. Cetron, president of Forecasting International, Ltd. The extraordinary capabilities of today's personal computers, when compared to the mainframe computers of just a few short years ago, are revolutionizing both business and accounting practices. Those extraordinary capabilities, moreover, are available at lower and lower cost. The computing power that cost over $4 million in a mainframe in 1972 cost approximately $15,000 in a mini-computer in 1982 and only a few thousand in microcomputer form by 1985—a drop that puts computing power within reach of the individual practitioner and small firm as well as the giants of the profession.

And it isn't the desktop personal computer alone. There is micro-mainframe interface technology, permitting direct access to client data. There is increasingly sophisticated software designed to perform multiple functions, and data bases containing volumes of readily accessible information. There are laptop computers to take along on audit engagements. There are modems to transmit data over telephone lines. There are local area networks and multi-user systems and management information systems from the relatively simple to the enormously complex. And the computer revolution has just begun. Artificial intelligence, as an example, is just in its infancy, with potential as yet unrealized. How will both business and accounting change when machines can use judgment?

Even now, however, the computer revolution has led to a brave new world. In a matter of hours today's "CPA can develop break-even analyses, cash-flow projections, budgets and merger analyses," Robert S. Roussey of Arthur Andersen wrote in the *Journal of Accountancy* in 1986, "all of which used to take days or weeks using mainframe or time-sharing computers, if they were done at all." Almost any service a CPA renders has been both speeded and enhanced by computerization. But change breeds further change. "The widespread use of computers is changing the traditional client-CPA relationship," the AICPA Future Issues Committee reported in 1984, "expanding the scope of services, fostering competition, and creating changes in the operating structure of CPA firms and businesses generally. Within the next two decades, the increasingly rapid growth in computer and information technology is expected to revolutionize business practice in all areas and to create a host of new products and services."

Even before these new products and services burst on the scene, the technological revolution is having a major impact on the three traditional practice areas of audit, tax, and management advisory services. It will lead, inevitably, to new definitions of traditional service and to totally new areas of service. It will also, in the long run, have an impact on the day-to-day work that CPAs do, both in public practice and in industry, and on the structure of firms.

Audit

The impact of technology on audit practice ranges from modest to dramatic, says the AICPA EDP Technology Research Subcommittee. Right now, on what might be called the low end of the impact scale, audits can be performed in the traditional way using a micro-computer as a super calculator. "We've taken mechanical things, the pencil, and fourteen-column paper," says William Gladstone, chairman of Arthur Young, "and automated them." On the high end of the scale, in the future, technology may well change what is audited, as well as how.

Technology can be expected to affect the audit process in many ways. Future audits will be more effective and efficient. They may depart entirely from financial statements as we know them today.

Computer-based audits are more effective. They can contain more analytical review because the micro-computer enables the auditor to make cost-effective calculations and statistical analyses without the manual drudgery previously required. The computer also permits the preparation of projections, which can then be easily compared with actual results. There is already a growing emphasis on forecasts, as noted in Chapter 6; increasing computerization may well accelerate this trend.

Computer-induced efficiency will reduce audit costs. Because micro-computers process vast amounts of data quickly and accurately, most clerical tasks can be eliminated in both the client's and the auditor's offices. Hourly costs will, therefore, be reduced. Equipment costs, as we've seen, are coming down. Data storage costs may come down as well, as disk storage becomes commonplace. With reduced costs, and audit bringing in a smaller portion of firm revenue, either the audit itself will have to be expanded or additional client services will have to be developed.

Computer-based audits may well become "real-time" audits, rather than periodic monitoring of financial statements, as corporations extend their databases to become reporting vehicles. Periodic financial statements may well become obsolete, in other words, if auditors and securities analysts and other interested parties can tap directly into corporate databases for instantaneous information. If this happens, "the nature of what we now call auditing by the year 2000 is going to be substantially different from what it is at the present time," says Duane Kullberg, chairman of Arthur Andersen, "a real-time monitoring system as opposed to periodic auditing." What this means, in turn, is that instead of attesting to the reliability of financial statements, auditors may be called upon to attest to the reliability of the database system and its controls. Instead of attesting only to the reliability of financial information, whether in statement or database form, auditors can expect to be called on to attest to the reliability of many other kinds of information. "Because the concept of independent verification of information for the benefit of third parties is not specific to financial statements," notes Bob Elliott, "the auditor's skills also have enhanced value in the information age. In other words, an auditor is not simply a person who audits financial statements; he or she is a person who assures the veracity of any sufficiently objective information."

A new auditing opportunity that has already presented itself, and is likely to grow, is the certification of computer software and hardware systems. Other auditing opportunities range from labor data for union contract negotiations to cost justification for a utility rate increase to audience and circulation data for broadcast and print media. All of these types of audits have been conducted before; the computer will expand their reach.

Artificial intelligence, a computer simulation of the human thinking process, is no longer restricted to science fiction. It is clearly on the horizon and, equally clearly, will affect accounting practice. Expert systems, for example, are one aspect of artificial intelligence. Incorporating human knowledge into a data base, expert systems permit inexperienced people to solve problems and make decisions with the skill of the experienced. "They follow the problem-solving approach that a human expert would be likely to follow," says a 1986 draft report on artificial intelligence prepared by the AICPA's EDP Technology Research Subcommittee, "by breaking a problem down into its elements, looking for patterns in available information related to the problem, combining conclusions regarding individual problem elements, and eventually arriving at the conclusion that seems to have the most evidence in its favor." Already in use in other disciplines for diagnosing malfunctions in equipment and certain types of disease in humans, expert systems will be developed for specific accounting and auditing tasks. It's only a matter of time. Once in use, as Clifford E. Graese of Peat Marwick put it in the firm magazine, artificial intelligence "will permit accounting firms to harness the collective judgments of their best experts in each field for auditors to use on engagements to challenge their own thinking. While the individual auditor will still be responsible for determining the best approach in a given set of circumstances, expert systems will serve as tools for measuring his or her judgments."

Many technological developments are yet to come. Some, such as artificial intelligence, raise serious questions. "Many of the problems solved by CPAs do not involve a readily determinable 'right' answer," notes the EDP subcommittee's draft report on artificial intelligence, and it can take some time before a "wrong" answer is detected. If a human auditor defers to a computer, and the computer is later proven wrong, what happens? Conversely, if a human professional overrides the computer, and makes an erroneous decision, what happens? In either situation, the human could wind up in a precarious legal position.

Cross-checking and quality review, normally practiced by CPA firms, will be more important than ever. Quality control may even be aided by expert systems, if the firm's standards are built in to the program so that key questions must be addressed before decisions are made. But other issues remain. "What judgments will be made by a computer and not by a person?" asks Paula Cholmondeley, chairperson of the AICPA Future Issues Committee, which recently added artificial intelligence to its list of issues to be addressed by the profession. "How do you audit an expert system if a client puts one in?"

While we await the practical application of expert systems, significant technological progress has already been made in audit procedures. Many firms are developing their own software programs. AY/ASQ, for example, is Arthur Young's "Audit Smarter, Quicker," integrated software designed to automate the audit. With it, says Bill Gladstone, an auditor might, "plan an audit of cash, with the micro listing a series of questions about company controls. The auditor can determine whether the controls are strong or weak, and the screen will then display appropriate procedures." The program walks the auditor through the entire audit, helping make and support decisions, so that even inexperienced auditors can benefit from "partner-level thinking." At the same time, the program doesn't make automatons of auditors. The auditor can use his or her judgment and override the program.

Tax

Just as the ideal audit of the future may be based on real-time information, says Bob Elliott, the same may happen on the tax front. "We could do away with periodic tax returns," he suggests, "and both report information and take taxes out in real time."

This development isn't yet at hand—and I'm not sure taxpayers eagerly look forward to the day when it is—but other manifestations of the technological era are clearly in the works. Already, tax professionals are keeping up to date with the complex world of taxes via electronic tax-reporting services. Then there's electronic filing, with direct transmission of taxpayer data, over telephone lines, from tax preparer to the IRS. According to Roscoe L. Egger, Jr., a consultant with Price Waterhouse who was commissioner of internal revenue from 1981 to 1986, electronic filing is "clearly the wave of the future." In 1986 the Internal Revenue Service conducted pilot projects in electronic filing in three locations; in 1987 the study was extended to seven additional locations. Within three to five years, says Egger, electronic filing will probably be a national reality.

Electronic filing, even in its pilot stages, has reduced errors and speeded refunds. But there are other wrinkles.

In 1987, the IRS expected to introduce "electronic re-funds," with refunds deposited directly into a taxpayer's checking or savings account via electronic fund transfer (EFT). Later on, according to John L. Wedick, Jr., IRS assistant commissioner of planning, finance, and research, writing in the *Journal of Accountancy*, "We may extend EFT to let taxpayers pay the amounts shown on balance-due returns with debit cards. . . . By the mid-1990's," he concludes, "the Internal Revenue Service wants to be able to receive and process a return filed electronically from anywhere in the world."

What does all this mean for certified public accoun-tants? It may mean increasing competition, as non-CPAs can make use of rapidly developing low-cost technology to make greater inroads into tax practice. It has already put pressure on fees, as clients question high fees for computer-generated returns. It may eventually, therefore, lead CPAs away from pure tax return preparation and into a higher level of tax practice, a level that may be aided by the development of artificial intelligence. Such a computer program, the EDP subcommittee predicts, "will have ac-cess and instant recall of all of the IRS codes, regulations, court cases and rulings. By following the rules of experts interviewed to program the expert system, it will have access to an almost infinite number of experiences from actual practice." With the aid of such a system, CPAs will be even better equipped to undertake complex analyses and to render expert tax advice.

Management Advisory Services

This fast-growing area, which includes the development of management information systems for clients, is clearly affected by technological change. Technological develop-ments themselves afford the opportunity to offer more services, to train client personnel, to provide sophisticated support for decision-making. With computers, the CPA—in small firm as well as large—can build financial models of a client's business, use spreadsheets for variable projections, and analyze a range of "what if" scenarios.

We've also reached the point, the EDP subcommittee suggests, where a "technical information systems background will have to be blended with micro-computer applications expertise, stronger communications skills and broader perspective to grasp the client's systems from an information management perspective." Technical expertise is no longer enough. MAS consultants will need wide-ranging skills and the ability to apply them to meet diverse client needs.

Firm Structure

Technological advances may lead, of necessity, to changes in the traditional structure of public accounting firms. Those advances, it must be remembered, affect both CPAs and their clients. As CPAs use computers to process information, fewer entry-level professional people and more para-professionals may be needed. As Larry D. Horner, chairman and chief executive of Peat Marwick, points out, an audit of a major bank in the mid-1960's required more than a thousand people on the first day, just to gather information; the same audit, conducted today, uses a handful of people throughout the year to do the same work. As clients increasingly turn to computers to manage their own financial affairs, similarly, they may no longer need CPAs for routine chores. Even now, many routine information-gathering chores connected with audits are performed by internal audit staff aided by computerized data.

Technological progress, as a result, has a number of implications for firm staffing and structure. Firms will still need raw recruits, but they may not need as many of them; with fewer hires firms will have to increase efforts to retain the people they need. This may not be difficult, since entry-level work is likely to be more challenging than it has been in the past. As computers become standard equipment, drudge work by junior auditors—the manual checking of seemingly endless quantities of data—should soon be a thing of the past. At the same time, says Pete Scanlon, chairman of Coopers & Lybrand, "The work that teaches the mechanics and discipline of the audit process won't be there any more. . . . The focus will need to be on training of a more advanced, more technical level."

With fewer people at the bottom, and a growing need for middle-level managers, the result will be a shift from the pyramid-shaped structure accounting firms have tradition-ally maintained to what Scanlon calls a cylinder. If, in-stead of a firm being built on a solid base of junior accountants, the personnel bulge moves to the middle, to the managerial level, what happens in the race to partner? Scanlon doesn't see a problem. "There is no finite number of partners," he says. "The world is becoming more com-plex, business is relying more on outside experts, and opportunities are unlimited."

Not everyone is so optimistic. More and more firms, some observers suspect, will move toward incorporation as a substitute for the partnership structure that has been prevalent in most states. Many problems need to be worked out, but Ron Weiner of New Jersey-based Weiner & Co. suggests that "people won't pressure to become partners" if they are given shares of the corporation. A corporate structure may be helpful in other areas as well. In states where it is permitted, CPAs are finding that operating as a commercial corporation can provide some protection against liability. Moreover, as Leonard Dopkins of Dopkins & Co. in Buffalo, New York, points out, the corporate form can help the flow of capital in accounting firms just as it did in investment banking firms, once run as partnerships using the capital of wealthy men and now virtually all incorporated.

It will take changes in state laws before CPA firms can operate as corporations everywhere. Whether or not those laws are passed, and whether or not firms choose to change their structure, says futurist Michael H. Annison, "The hierarchical way of looking at firms has to change, and productivity must be reevaluated."

Part of that reevaluation is under way, visible in the changing nature of CPA client services. "Rather than doing the client's work himself," notes Marvin Cetron, "the CPA's role is changing to that of a facilitator or resource person assisting in the client's financial training and development. This could involve, for instance, training clients in the application of computer software (such as spreadsheets) to the preparation of their own budgets, projections, and financial reports. . . . Where the cost of hiring a CPA firm to do the work would be prohibitive, the idea of doing the actual work themselves after CPA training is proving to be a feasible alternative for smaller client firms." The CPA, in short, will be even more of a management adviser.

If this is the case, then staff must be recruited and trained and used differently. Accounting recruits of the future are going to need computer skills. They are also going to need analytical skills, the ability to reason and to make decisions, even more than they do today. Education for accountants, as we've already discussed, must change to meet these changing needs. It must also change to meet the needs of an increasingly global profession.

Global Business/Global Accounting

The technological revolution is also speeding the internationalization of both business and accounting. "What has happened in the past five years is a true internationalization of the credit markets," Fred Zuckerman, treasurer of the Chrysler Corporation, told *The New York Times* in October 1986. Corporate financial officers find it as easy to raise capital in London as in New York, securities are traded virtually around the clock as stock exchanges around the world span time zones, overseas financial markets have been deregulated, and American investment banking is expanding overseas. "The pace of global investment has quickened dramatically," says Larry Horner, "thanks to the growth of multinational financing intermediaries and an electronic money market that can move billions of dollars anywhere in the world, literally at the press of a button."

This globalization of the capital markets is an ongoing and, thanks to technology, accelerating process. "In 1880 the world economy was only 10 percent integrated. In 1950 it was 25 percent integrated. In 1986," Joe Connor of Price Waterhouse told the Swiss-American Chamber of Commerce that year, "the figure is 50 percent. Some estimates have this integration increasing to as much as 75 percent by the year 2000."

Globalization also has significant implications. "The Capital Explosion: A Worldwide Quest for Money," a 1986 study by the Naisbitt Group for the international accounting firm Klynveld Main Goerdeler, found corporations tapping worldwide sources of capital in search of better financial terms, currency and stock exchange deregulation signaling new volatility in capital markets, and investment activity in Europe and the Third World accelerating as technology provides equal access to financial information. The result, in an echo of Connor's comments, is an interdependency of capital markets hitherto unknown. The study forecast that this interdependency will continue and become even more acute, with continuing improvements in communications increasing investment activity in both Europe and developing countries, a global twenty-four-hour stock market within the next few years, and an overhaul of the world monetary system. Campbell Corfe of KMG notes that the pace of change is accelerating as we build toward a global economy.

As business and finance become international in scope, so, of necessity, do the public accounting firms that serve them. All of the major national firms have overseas operations. Some smaller firms do as well, sometimes through associations of CPA firms that link domestic and foreign firms in a cooperative network. The DKF Accountancy Group, for example, has an extensive international network with over 150 offices in nearly fifty countries. The International Affiliation of Independent Accounting Firms and the International Group of Accounting Firms also have strong international networks. And the National Conference of CPA Practitioners has formed a loose affiliation with the Association of Practicing Accountants in Great Britain, as the International Conference of Accounting Practitioners.

Services offered by international public accounting firms parallel the services offered by domestic firms in audit, tax and management consulting. But the expanding global economy is having an impact on traditional accounting services. "Accounting practices will be revised and new ones introduced to accommodate a dizzying array of innovative investment instruments being developed in international markets," the Naisbitt report concludes.

Right now, as an example, Touche Ross International (TRI) lists some of its fundamental tax services as corporate tax planning, international tax planning, the fiscal consequences of floating foreign currencies, foreign tax credits, and tax equalization for citizens working abroad. In a specific example, TRI advised a U.S. corporation on tax planning for European investment, giving particular emphasis to intercompany pricing, special incentives, and enterprise zones offering tax advantages. Arthur Young International (AYI), similarly, offers diverse management support services to meet the needs of multinational businesses: helping new companies draft business plans, set up internal accounting systems, and determine ways of funding future growth; and helping established concerns implement information systems, plan acquisitions and mergers, and structure joint ventures. For example, when a large U.S. insurance broker acquired a diversified organization headquartered in the United Kingdom, AYI assisted the new owner in disposing of a retailing operation that did not fit his corporate strategy; its assistance ranged from structuring the deal to the closing.

As the international world of finance gets smaller and smaller, "our clients are looking to us for far more than the traditional services of prospectuses and reviews of companies engaged in merger negotiations," KMG notes in its introduction to the Naisbitt report. "In addition to requests for solving the complex accounting problems arising from the use of sophisticated financial instruments and interpreting financial statements in one country for investors in another country, we encountered broad questions on financial structures as well as the who, how, when, and why of international financing." In the next decade, if the global economy develops as anticipated, "changes in the global economy will continue to alter the operations of accounting firms. In particular, the growth of the service economy will give rise to new accounting procedures that give service-based industries better access to capital."

Growth may also give rise to new structures for international accounting firms. Right now, structures vary. Arthur Andersen, for example, is a centralized worldwide entity. This has advantages, says AA, because in "a truly cohesive international organization . . . the parts [are treated] as segments of the whole . . . not as individual operations with a loose tie to the larger organization." Other firms, such as Touche Ross, are decentralized, with "member firms . . . united in one cooperative organization." This decentralized approach has advantages, too, because local firms provide expert local advice yet are linked together in an international network for international clients. As Bill Gladstone of Arthur Young, another decentralized firm, put it: "We may have twenty-five hundred people in Holland, with a great firm name which we won't change, but when we work together we use the Arthur Young name for international clients."

These different structures become both visible and important as, in what may be a sign of the future, mergers are making large firms larger still. Effective April 1, 1987, Peat Marwick International and Kynveld Main Goerdeler, two of the world's largest firms, became the world's largest, to be known internationally as Klynveld Peat Marwick Goerdeler (KPMG). In the United States, where Peat Marwick Mitchell (founded in 1897) has been far stronger than KMG Main Hurdman (which was created by merger, itself, less than a decade ago), the combined firm is Peat Marwick; for legal purposes, on audit documents, it will be KPMG Peat Marwick Main & Co. With PMI's strength in the United States, KMG's strength in Europe, and their combined strength worldwide, the new firm, totaling some fifty-eight thousand in staff, will be a forceful presence on the international scene. That is, it will be after it succeeds in merging two disparate corporate cultures. Many observers note that difficulties are bound to arise, at least in part because KMG has been a loose international confederation of autonomous firms while Peat Marwick International has had far more centralized leadership. At this writing, although the merger is reasonably solid in the United States, the United Kingdom, and the Netherlands, a few partnership groups have dropped out and others are sitting on the fence. Negotiations continue in a number of countries. It could take some time before blended operations run smoothly. When they do, however, the world's largest accounting firm will be a force to be reckoned with.

International Standards

As the world economy becomes both more complex and increasingly interrelated, with more and more companies seeking capital and selling products and services across national borders, financial reporting lags behind. In fact, Larry Horner believes that "conflicting national standards and acceptable accounting approaches—and the wide spectrum of economic and political concerns they represent—have begun to pose obstacles to the free and orderly movement of capital across national borders." If cross-border investment is to increase, as an inevitable part of the integration of the world economy, standardized accounting and auditing practices may be required. Such standardization does not, as yet, exist. Right now, as the Naisbitt report puts it, "corporate balance sheets [are] virtually incomprehensible outside domestic borders."

There are similarities. U.S. accounting and auditing standards have had a noticeable influence on worldwide standards. This is because, along with the United Kingdom's, they may be the most highly developed standards in the world. It is also because U.S. business has had a marked influence on the rest of the world. "This was particularly true during the heady days of the fifties and sixties when the U.S. was riding high in international trade and finance," former FASB board member Ralph E. Walters has written. "It is a simple demonstration of the golden rule—he who has the gold makes the rules." Capital was flowing outward from the United States then, followed by the major U.S. firms with their overseas subsidiaries, and the U.S. accounting and auditing standards. Today the situation has changed, with capital flowing across the oceans in both directions, but U.S. standards are still the most pervasive. National standards in a great many countries, as Walters puts it, "bear the heavy imprint of U.S. influence."

Yet there are also many exceptions, a variety of accounting practices in use around the globe. It's not particularly surprising that nation-by-nation practices differ. After all, the objectives and purposes of financial reporting vary from country to country. In some places, financial reporting is primarily for the benefit of labor unions and employees; in other places the primary users are seen as investors and creditors. In countries where government sets the rules, financial reporting is frequently directed toward tax collection. As Joe Connor notes, "Cultures and economies and tax laws and legal systems differ radically, leading to differences in national accounting standards. . . . There are basic differences on fundamental matters, such as deferred taxes, consolidation of subsidiaries, disclosure, inflation-adjusted versus historic costs."

There are even differences on the definitions of such basic terms as assets and earnings and depreciation and reserves, differences that can have a profound effect on the corporate bottom line. "For example," Larry Horner told the British-American Chamber of Commerce, "differences in reporting depreciation boosted British Oxygen Group's 1983 earnings from £55 million under British rules to £93 million under U.S. rules. Likewise, differing treatment of deferred taxes cut British Telcom's 1984 earnings by 43 percent—from $1.4 billion to $790 million—when reports were translated from British to U.S. accounting. And we're talking now about two systems that came from a common ancestor just one hundred years ago! Elsewhere," Horner continues, "the translation problems can be even worse. For example, setting up hidden reserves to smooth out year-to-year earnings swings is considered sound practice in Germany and Switzerland, where investors put a premium on earnings stability. Under U.S. rules, which emphasize disclosure, such reserves are strictly prohibited. As a result, you're likely to see far wider earnings differences under U.S. rules. . . . An American investor who pays what he thinks is a reasonable price-to-earnings multiple for a foreign stock may find out that he's paid a far higher price when earnings are restated in accordance with U.S. accounting rules.''

Many people focus on the differences. Ralph Walters looks at the similarities. In his view, we can probably never have absolutely uniform standards for all, but we should be able to attain 90 percent uniformity, with specialized standards or implementation in some areas. "The differences are not all that great," he insists. "When you get down to it, there are more similarities than differences—money is money, cash is cash, money comes in, goes out, you have income, have expenses, and something left over. . . ."

Right now corporations *do* conduct business across international borders. Investors *do* make investments across the same lines. And accounting, which is indeed the international language of business and finance, must move toward internationally accepted standards. Not a single standard, necessarily, which may be impossible to achieve, but, as Horner suggests, a common set of standards that would give investors anywhere in the world the opportunity to compare results reported under the same accounting conventions.

Movement is under way. It's slow—"it's like molasses in January," says Ralph Walters, currently a U.S. representative on the International Accounting Standards Committee (IASC)—but there is movement. The IASC and the International Federation of Accountants (IFAC), including representatives from ninety-nine accountancy bodies in seventy-four countries, jointly represent the accounting profession worldwide. IASC develops accounting standards for the private sector. IFAC gets involved in everything else, setting standards for audit, ethics, and education; it has recently formed a group to look into standards for governmental accounting and auditing. IASC, meanwhile, has issued some two dozen pronouncements on international accounting standards, covering such subjects as depreciation, pension benefits, and the treatment of long-term investments.

Neither IFAC nor IASC has enforcement powers, and their pronouncements meet with varying degrees of acceptance. But some countries, and some multinational corporations, have adopted the standards. By and large, notes Walters, the less developed the country, the more international standards are accepted; "they don't have historical baggage to cope with, are happy to have someone else set standards." The converse is also true; the more developed the country, the less likely it is to accept. Among developed countries, in Walters' view, Canada has probably done the most toward accepting international standards. Its Institute of Chartered Accountants, he reports, works closely with the Ontario Securities Commission and the Toronto Stock Exchange, which have encouraged registrants to comply with international standards. On the auditing front, according to Bob Sempier, executive director of IFAC, Australia has determined that anything on the IFAC agenda will not be added to its own; instead IFAC guidelines will be treated as an exposure draft, released to members for comment, and then enacted. This is "a significant breakthrough," says Sempier, "on the part of a developed country."

The U.S. is another story. There are few differences between what has been issued domestically and what has been issued internationally in auditing standards, Sempier notes, so adherence to one generally means adherence to the other. But international accounting standards, by and large, while they accommodate U.S. generally accepted accounting principles, are not as tight. To gain any acceptance, it's been deemed necessary to start with a standard that sets a range of acceptable practices, with the objective over time to narrow the range and come down eventually to one acceptable accounting standard. This is a weakness, as Walters notes, because, although it eliminates extremes of practice, it tends to perpetuate diversity. But politics being what they are, and people being what they are, it may simply not be possible to impose a single rigid standard all at once.

Back in 1983, when Ralph Walters was completing his term on the Financial Accounting Standards Board and before he got involved in international standard-setting, he issued a plea for attention to international harmonization of accounting standards. Today, he says, nothing has changed. "The SEC and the U.S. exchanges pay nothing but lip service to the concept. The principal attitude in the U.S. is inattention."

That's not entirely true. The FASB, while continuing to emphasize its primary concern with standard-setting in the United States to meet U.S. needs, does maintain liaison with standard-setting bodies in other countries and on the international scene. The FASB chairman has attended IASC meetings and has met with representatives of the United Kingdom and Canada. But internationally uniform standards are not exactly a burning issue in the United States, and considerably more effort may be necessary if they are to become a reality. More people—including users and preparers of financial statements—will have to become involved. As a first step in this direction the International Coordinating Committee of Financial Analysts Associations recently joined the board of IASC, the first non–accountants organization to do so. Robert L. May, president of IFAC, hopes that management accountants, the preparers of financial statements who represent some 58 percent of the world's accountants, will also become involved.

The pressures are building. More and more companies have multinational listings—some 475 or 500, according to Corfe—and are looking to multinational accounting standards. Without them, duplicate financial statements are sometimes required as a foreign-based company, for example, wants to register with the SEC and must therefore conform to U.S. standards. As Connor points out, "market forces which assess financial data are causing unrelenting pressure for more conformity." But, he goes on, "uniform standards are highly desirable, difficult to achieve." On a more determined note, Horner says, "As long as earnings means are arrived at one way in New York and a different way in London, we're not going to make much progress in bringing our world economy—and the opportunities it holds—much closer together. What we need are full, fair, and comparable disclosure of financial reports with the objective and rigorous international standards developed by the world's accountants through their organization, the IASC."

Other groups, meanwhile, are also working toward international harmonization of accounting principles. The United Nations and the Organization for Economic Cooperation and Development have expressed interest. The American Accounting Association and KMG cosponsored a 1986 Conference on Standard-Setting for Financial Reporting. And the European Economic Community is issuing and enforcing uniform accounting rules as part of removing barriers to intra-Community trade in the creation of a common market. Three EEC Directives have been issued to date; others are under consideration. Unlike IASC standards, which have all the force of suggestion, the EEC Directives have the force of law. Each is issued with a deadline for implementation. If a member state does not respect the deadline, it is reminded by the Commission; if reminders do not work, the state can be taken before the European Court of Justice.

The 1986 EEC Update reports:

- The Fourth Directive, which has had a profound impact on accounting in most member states, is designed to establish "minimum equivalent legal requirements as regards the extent of the financial information that should be made available to the public by companies that are in competition with one another." It gives specific direction on layout of the balance sheet, valuation rules, information that must be disclosed in the notes, etc. But its overriding principle is that "annual accounts must give a true and fair view of the company's assets, liabilities, financial position and profit or loss." This may not seem controversial. But it took almost ten years of negotiation before this directive was adopted, perhaps in part because for many EEC member states "the introduction of the overriding principle of 'true and fair view' is new."

It's taken still more years to translate adoption into action. The deadline for implementing this directive was July 31, 1980. By mid-1986 eight member states had passed appropriate legislation; three had been brought before the European Court of Justice. One of the three, Italy, was condemned by the Court in March 1986 and, at this writing, was preparing a draft bill.

- The Seventh Directive, dealing with consolidated accounts, took almost seven years of long-drawn-out discussions to resolve. The reason: Where consolidated accounts were in use at all in member states, there were two very different approaches to the concept. One dealt with consolidation based on an economic group, on centrally managed enterprises. The other dealt with consolidation in terms of legal control, of majority voting power. The Commission, after initially leaning the other way, eventually selected legal power of control as the basis of consolidation.
- The Eighth Directive, adopted in April 1984, deals with the educational and professional qualifications of auditors. It sets forth educational and experience requirements and states that independence is absolutely essential. It does not, to the disappointment of many, deal with mutual recognition of qualifications across national borders.

These directives, and others yet to come, are smoothing the way toward uniform financial reporting by transnational companies, at least within the European Economic Community. Since all EEC countries are also members of IFAC and IASC, they may also, in the long run, have some influence beyond Europe.

As the international aspects of the world economy grow, international accounting will inevitably if slowly move toward harmonization. Right now, it's "ahead of its time. Down the road, people will wake up and say we need international standards," Ralph Walters says, "and we can then say, we have them; they may need tightening, but we do have them." When that day comes, accounting, which has always been the language of business, will be a truly international language.

Summary: Where Do We Go From Here?

Certified Public Accountants: Certified means qualified, by virtue of passing an examination, and thereby approved by the state. Public relates to the special trust placed in CPAs to serve the public interest. Accountants are those men and women who prepare and review financial statements, do tax planning and tax return preparation, consult with clients on all manner of personal and business problems.

A narrow definition of a narrow job? Hardly. As we've seen throughout this book, the function of the CPA is only as limited as the needs of the CPA's clients, and the role of the CPA is changing and expanding along with the pursuits of American and international business.

The ranks of CPAs are growing, as more and more men and women are attracted to this ever-more-challenging career—a challenge that is not limited to the practice of public accounting. Only about half of current AICPA membership is now employed in public practice, while members in industry run a close second.

Regardless of the makeup of AICPA membership, in any case, many traditionalists point to the *P* in CPA and remind anyone who will listen that the *P* stands for "Public" and that CPAs, by virtue of their license, have a unique responsibility to the public. That responsibility, as we've seen, is customarily defined by the audit. In response, some members in industry, such as John Meinert

223

of Hartmarx and Ian A. McConnachie, president of Americanuck Incorporated, suggest a change of name to Certified Professional Accountant. But it's unlikely that a name change would have much substantive impact, since the profession and its organizations have always revolved around the standards, codes, and rules of public accounting. There have been few comparable standards, codes, and rules on the industry side—although this may change as the Anderson proposals extend codes and rules to all Institute members. In any event, CPA, as in Certified Public Accountant, is a title that earns great respect. It isn't likely to be changed.

But the thought behind the suggestion is worth pondering for a moment because "public" can be interpreted in different ways. In a narrow sense, it refers to the rendering of opinions on financial statements so that those statements are worthy of public confidence. In a broader sense, it means, in Ian McConnachie's words, "the responsibility of accountants to the general public (citizens, investors, members of the securities industries, credit grantors, or any member of the public who has reason to read a financial statement)." Such a broad definition takes in both the preparers of those statements, in industry, and the auditors of those statements, in public practice. It includes those who account for government spending, as well as those who audit public funds. And it encompasses those who do research in accounting and auditing, and who pass the fruits of their research on to others in classrooms and conference centers.

This pubic trust is the essence of certified public accounting and will continue to be at its heart as the profession changes and grows in response to a changing society. Existing skills may be redefined. New areas of specialization may develop. A broader range of services may be offered. And all of us—as taxpayers, employees, investors, businesspeople, and just plain citizens—have a stake in what certified public accountants do and the way that they do it.

Index